The Complete Guide to
North American
FRESHWATER
GAME
FISHING

The Complete Guide to

North American
Freshwater
Game
Fishing

Henry Waszczuk
and Italo Labignan

FOREWORD BY
Ron Lindner
PUBLISHER
IN-FISHERMAN COMMUNICATIONS NETWORK

KEY PORTER BOOKS

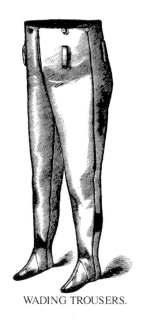

WADING TROUSERS.

The decorative archival drawings are from *Great Fishing Tackle Catalogs of the Golden Age*, edited by Samuel Melner and Hermann Kessler, and are reproduced with permission from Lyons & Burford Publishers.

Canadian Cataloguing in Publication Data

Waszczuk, Henry, 1950-
    The Complete Guide to North American
    Freshwater Game Fishing

Includes index.
ISBN 1-55013-385-3 (cloth)   1-55013-613-5 (pbk)

1. Fishing – North America. 2. Freshwater fishes – North America. I. Labignan, Italo, 1956 – II. Title.

SH462.W37 1992 799.1'1'097 C91-095472-0

Key Porter Books Limited
70 The Esplanade
Toronto, Ontario
Canada M5E 1R2

Distributed in the United States of America by:
National Book Network, Inc.

Design: Dreadnaught
Fish illustrations: Joe Hertnett
Maps: Dave McKay
Typesetting: MACTRIX DTP
Printed and bound in Hong Kong

94 95 96 97 98 99 6 5 4 3 2 1

FRONTISPIECE:

FEW ANGLERS CAN RESIST THE LURE OF THE OPEN WATER.

OPPOSITE:

A FLY-FISHER SAVORS THE GLORY OF AN EARLY MORNING ON A REMOTE NORTHERN LAKE.

Contents

Foreword / 6
Introduction / 8
A Brief History of Angling / 10
Catch and Release / 20

Arctic Char / 34
Arctic Grayling / 38
Atlantic Salmon / 42
Brook Trout / 48
Brown Trout / 53
Channel Catfish / 58
Chinook Salmon / 64
Chum Salmon / 70
Coho Salmon / 75
Crappie / 80
Cutthroat Trout / 84
Dolly Varden / 88
Inconnu / 92
Kokanee / 96
Lake Trout / 100
Largemouth Bass / 106
Muskellunge / 110
Perch / 114
Pickerel / 120
Pike / 124

Pink Salmon / 130
Rainbow Trout / 134
Rock Bass / 138
Sauger / 142
Smallmouth Bass / 146
Sockeye Salmon / 152
Steelhead / 158
Striped Bass / 162
Sturgeon / 166
Sunfish / 170
Walleye / 174
White Bass / 178

Glossary / 182
Index / 190

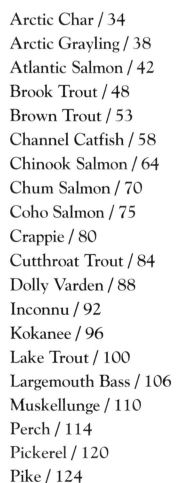

Foreword

OPPOSITE:

THE AUTHORS

WITH A CATCH.

Sportfishing means different things to different people. For some, it is simply a means of relaxation, an excuse to "get away from it all" or to spend time with friends and loved ones. For others, such as tournament-minded fishermen, it offers a field of competition where the angler has to beat not only the fish, but also the other contestants. For some, fishing is an obsession, something they need in steady doses in order to feel good. For others, namely fishing guides and other angling pros, the sport is work, a way to earn a living. The list of reasons why people go fishing goes on and on.

Underlying this wide variety of personal motivations for fishing is one common denominator: the desire to catch fish. This objective is really the bottom line after all else is stripped away. Henry Waszczuk and Italo Labignan have chosen to make a career of assisting the sport fisherman to achieve this goal, offering techniques for catching fish. They have succeeded admirably. Firm believers in the power of education, they have been unstinting in their efforts to provide anglers with useful knowledge about sportfishing. Their methods have been described as multimedia since they use books, magazines, videos, seminars, expositions, and television programs in their teaching. These varied means have all led to a single end: easily understood systems and tactics designed for only one thing – catching fish. And whether you're young or old, a novice or a veteran, a fanatic or an occasional angler, catching fish is, after all, what it's all about.

Ron J. Lindner

Introduction

North America, with its freshwater lakes, streams, and rivers, is home to hundreds of freshwater-fish species of every description and size. Angling for these fish has become a booming leisure activity for millions of North Americans, young and old. Our *Canadian Sportfishing* team has had the rare good fortune to fish in numerous parts of this continent and to become familiar with many fish species. During these fishing trips for our television shows, books, and magazine articles, we have accumulated a large body of experience that we would like to share with you so that your fishing can become more productive and enjoyable.

Our experience also came in handy when it was time to choose the species to be showcased in this book. Our selection criteria went well beyond the conventional, narrow definitions of "game fish." How did we choose some species of fish over others? Size was a key factor – big fish are always interesting. Fighting qualities were also of prime importance, as well as public interest. For example, the sunfish family is very popular with countless anglers from all over North America. Another key factor was availability. We felt it was important to cover species that could be and would be encountered by average as well as dedicated anglers. Lastly, we felt that various underutilized species merited some exposure in this book – fish that were not well known but well worth fishing for. We hope we have achieved a pleasant and informative balance between traditional "game fish," and a few interesting and accessible "newcomers" as well. Angling is, after all, fun, and variety is the spice of life.

Our *Canadian Sportfishing* experience also taught us what kinds of information should be included for each species chosen for the book. Our aim was to give you more information that would enable you to become a better angler. One of the often frustrating realities of fishing for sport is the fact that

only a few anglers take most of the fish. Ever wonder why? Is it just simple luck? We think not. We believe that, to become successful, the angler has to do a bit of homework first. We've found that a little knowledge goes a long way, so we've put together an educational profile of each species featured in this book. From now on, you'll *know* your quarry.

There is detailed information on species identification, size limits and distribution, preferred habitats, spawning behavior, and unique dietary needs. Each species profile also includes an outline of fishing tackle and techniques, as well as special tips to give you that little bit of extra knowledge to "put you over the top."

North America offers the finest and most varied freshwater fishing in the world. We hope that this book will spark your interest in the art of angling and increase your appreciation for North America's freshwater fisheries. We know it will make you a better angler.

The authors would like to thank a very able and dedicated support staff, including Charlie McDonald, Craig Orr and Wolf Seefeld, for their many contributions which helped make this book possible.

We would also like to acknowledge some of our most important sources of information such as the In-Fisherman Handbook Series, the Hunting & Fishing Library by Dick Sternberg and the McClane's *New Standard Fishing Encyclopedia*. A special thanks to Dr. W.B. Scott and Dr. E.J. Crossman for their excellent work *Freshwater Fishes Of Canada* which was an invaluable source of information throughout the project.

NOTHING QUITE MATCHES THE THRILL OF HOOKING A LIVELY FISH!

A Brief History of Angling

North America's premier participation sport is undoubtedly angling. Yet, during its beginnings, angling had very little to do with sport and much to do with survival. Ancient peoples had to fish in order to eat. Challenge and sport had no place in fishing, and catch and release would have been viewed as sheer lunacy by prehistoric people (indeed, in many poverty-stricken areas of the world it is still viewed with disdain).

Much has changed since then. Now the sophisticated tournament angler rides in a bass boat. The implements are huge outboards, stealthy electric motors, graphite fishing rods, and large cases of fishing lures. Electronics are used to scan the water with sound waves and find the fish, and to measure water temperature, water acidity/alkalinity, and oxygen content. Little is left to chance. Modern anglers have advanced light-years beyond the wildest dreams of their early ancestors.

ANCIENT ORIGINS

The earliest methods of catching fish were strictly utilitarian, filling nutritional needs. There are indications that the earliest Paleolithic fishermen specialized in spearing fish stranded in pools after floods or tides receded. Although this technique was productive at times, it was essentially a haphazard way of subsisting. More reliable methods of capturing fish were eventually devised. As society advanced, so did fishing techniques. The concept of using hook and bait to catch fish was predated by the use of gorges and bait. A gorge was a rather nasty-looking affair, consisting of a long, thin splinter of bone that was imbedded in bait and attached to some form of line. When an unsuspecting fish swallowed

OPPOSITE:

MUCH OF YESTERYEAR'S FLY-FISHING KNOWLEDGE IS STILL VALID TODAY.

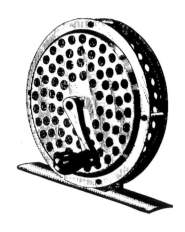

the bait, the bone and line slid easily into its stomach. A sharp tug of the hand line caused the bone gorge to jam across the stomach, and the fish could be retrieved. The hand lines were probably also attached to pieces of wood so they could be tossed farther out over the water to get as close to the fish as possible.

The first hooks were constructed from natural materials and certainly predated the manufacture of steel. Early civilizations used hooks made from such diverse materials as human or animal bones, cactus thorns, and even insect legs. Flint hooks were used in some societies long before bronze hooks came to be manufactured in more developed civilizations. In these early days of fishing, both live and dead baits were used for catching a variety of fish.

IMITATING NATURE

Angling took its next great leap during the heyday of Greek civilization – the introduction of imitation bait in the form of the artificial fly. This ingenious invention must have caused quite a stir among the many bait-fishermen of the day. Fly-fishing and the use of artificial lures can therefore be said to have evolved at the same time.

The next major historical angling developments occurred in the fifteenth century. According to accounts from this period, sportfishing rivaled fishing for food. One of the earliest written works on angling was the *Treatyse of Fishing with an Angle*, printed in 1496. It gives precise instructions for constructing homemade tackle. There are detailed descriptions of the manufacture of three-piece rods, which were used for bait- and fly-fishing. Even the manufacture of hooks (using an anvil, file, and steel needles) was detailed for the angler of that day. There is also a discussion about dyeing white horsehair line to match conditions for the different seasons. It is interesting to notice that modern anglers' preoccupation with color and its effects on fish was also shared by their predecessors. It's also surprising to see the degree of sophistication revealed in angling methods of the 1400s. The *Treatyse of Fishing with an Angle* describes bottom-fishing with weights for trout and coarse fish, as well as float-fishing and artificial fly-fishing. Even modern anglers would do well to read these old accounts, which contain many tips that are still useful. Some principles of fishing, such as keeping out of sight of the fish when stream-bank fishing or keeping the rod tip up when fighting a fish, are universal in their application.

LINE-RETRIEVAL IMPROVEMENTS

The angler's ingenuity soon turned to improving methods of retrieving line. It was no longer good enough to be restricted to whatever length of line would fit along the length of a rod. The need for greater line capacity became evident during the casting of lures in lakes where the fish were often farther offshore and in stream-fishing where flies were drifted some distance downstream, passing over potential fish lies. The first fishing reels (then more commonly known as winches) were invented in Britain between 1651 and 1655. Although the Chinese had reels 160 years earlier, there is very little knowledge of their development. Even today, reels are not always used, and the modern ice-fisherman will often simply wrap extra line around wooden or plastic line winders. Experts across the globe still use 12- to 20-foot rods with a minute length of line attached to the end. Brass "multiplier" reels were developed to allow line to be retrieved at a faster rate, yet the center-pin, single-action, float-fishing reels of today are remarkably similar to the reels of yesteryear.

FISHING LINE TECHNOLOGY

Fishing lines show a great diversity during their development history. During the 1500s, the British made lines of horsehair. A single horsehair was used for minnow-sized fish, several strands for trout, and more than a dozen for salmon. The horsehair lengths were knotted together to make the line as long as

A PADDLE, A ROD AND REEL, AND THE SPLENDOR OF NATURE.

needed. Even wire leaders were employed by yesterday's anglers for tooth-studded fish such as pike. Lines were also made from silk. In the late 1800s and early 1900s, catgut was used for its great strength. Even silkworm gut was used because of its strength and small diameter.

The development of fishing line has progressed considerably since the days of horsehair and silk. In spite of the great advances with high-tech, polymer lines, it is perhaps ironic that the old silk lines have actually enjoyed a bit of a nostalgic resurgence with the fly-fishing set.

One of the first "modern" fishing lines marketed in North America was Dacron line. It is a very supple line made of braided polyester fibers. Although it is still widely used today as fly-reel backing and for long-line trolling, monofilament line is preferred for its greater strength and reduced visibility.

Monofilament line is the result of chemical-engineering advances in the plastics industry. It actually consists of nylon, a synthetic made from polymers and resins. These lines come in a wide variety of breaking strengths, from 1- to more than 100-pound test.

Monofilament line's greatest drawback is its elasticity under tension, which leads to problems in setting the hook on fish and controlling them during the fight. When the angler raises the rod tip to set the hook, the stretch of the monofilament line reduces the force applied on the hook. Another problem is the ease with which monofilament line breaks when nicked. New developments with nylon lines may solve these problems.

SPACE-AGE FISHING RODS

Although cane poles are still used in many parts of North America, the introduction of new rod-building materials has given the modern angler a fantastic array of rod weights, actions, and prices to choose from. It's interesting, too, that the carefully manufactured split-cane rods are now much more expensive than their high-tech counterparts.

Rod building changed dramatically during the Second World War. Fiberglass technology grew, making it possible to manufacture light, flexible, yet durable and strong rods. Fiberglass rods could be turned out by machines at a much faster rate than by hand, thus lowering prices. Yet, these machine-made

models represented precision technology and boasted a beautifully tapered shape and superb action. Further refinements produced lighter rods, relegating nonfiberglass rods to museums or the attic. The dominance of fiberglass as the top rod-building material continued until the 1980s when new, even more advanced materials made their debut. Graphite, a material used in the aerospace industry, made its way onto the drawing boards and into production lines. Graphite was soon followed by still other "space-age" materials such as boron and, most recently, Kevlar. These materials were introduced in an effort to make rods lighter yet tougher. Obviously, an angler would have more enjoyment fishing with a rod that weighed 4 ounces than with one that weighed 8 ounces. Graphite rods are a dream compared to many of their older fiberglass equivalents.

Today, graphite and graphite/fiberglass composite rods have achieved prominence in the marketplace. Expensive rods contain a high percentage of

LIGHT- TO MEDIUM-ACTION SPINNING ROD-AND-REEL COMBOS, LIKE THESE BERKLEY AND ABU GARCIA PRODUCTS, ARE IDEAL FOR SMALLMOUTH FISHING.

graphite fibers, making them as light as possible without sacrificing strength. Prices are higher, but far from unreasonable. Most rods on the market today are actually graphite/fiberglass composites: graphite is used in small quantities in order to keep prices down. Usually the greater the percentage of graphite used, the lighter and more sensitive the rod will be (and, of course, the higher the price). Graphite/fiberglass rods often cost between $30 and $70 and are becoming increasingly popular.

In the "old days," fishing-rod selection was poor or nonexistent. Only the length and thickness of the rod varied. Today, rods are made from the lightest materials, producing a remarkably thin rod that is able to stand up to a lot of punishment. With the introduction of graphite, even the old, heavy-action muskie-trolling rods have become so light that the uninitiated often expect them to snap like toothpicks.

THE AGE OF SPECIALIZATION

Sophisticated manufacturing has produced an array of conventional rod sizes and actions, as well as some special rods for particular situations, for example, trolling and casting a variety of muskie lures. The jerk-bait rod, for example, has been designed for only the jerk bait. Bass rods are also specialized.

EACH YEAR MILLIONS OF DOLLARS ARE SPENT ON FISHING.

TERRY MCDONALD

Aside from the great variety of standard casting and spinning rods of various sizes and weights, special rods have made their debut, like the flipping rods, which are designed for making simple, underhand flip casts over very short distances. In fact, many of today's bass anglers use several rods, each designed with a certain lure presentation and situation in mind. It's not uncommon to see at least a couple of 5 1/2-foot bait casters in the boat. One rod might be baited with a shallow-running spinner bait, another with a topwater plug, and still another with a weedless plastic worm for fishing weed-choked areas. With such a selection of modern rods, the angler does not even need to waste time switching lures while fishing.

THE EVOLUTION OF LURES

One of the most fascinating aspects of fishing history is the development of lures. From the earliest days of bone gorges to the most sophisticated modern-day crankbaits, the story of lures can fill an entire book. Collections of old lures now rival stamp collections in value and interest.

Flies were the first lures to be developed. Animal hair and bird feathers were tied onto the earliest bronze hooks. Nature provided the inspiration and the materials to imitate a variety of aquatic, terrestrial, and airborne insects. Even though fly-tying now incorporates a great number of man-made materials, flies for fishing remain similar to their predecessors.

Lures have undergone a fascinating development. Many historians consider spoons, rather than flies, to be the first types of lures produced. Bronze was first cut to shape in an effort to replicate the appearance of a bait fish. And if you have ever had a look at a friend's homemade lures, they are probably quite similar to their ancient counterparts. During the mid-1800s, lure development took a significant turn as the first U.S. patent for a spinnerbait was submitted. At this time, hand-carved wooden lures were also being developed. The manufacturing of plugs began at the turn of the century, and plastic lures were developed in the 1920s. Lure development has, of course, continued and become big business. The modern angler can choose from a bewildering assortment of crankbaits, spinners, spinnerbaits, buzzbaits, and spoons. And, as if this were not enough, there is also a phenomenal array of jigs, plastic worms, twister tails, and many others.

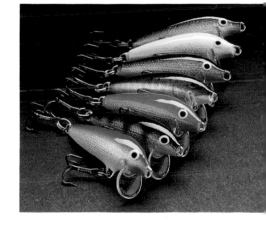

A RAINBOW OF SUPERB RAPALA PLUGS.

ELECTRONIC WIZARDRY

The latest developments in angling are in "high-tech" electronic gear. Sonar was, of course, drawn from the military technology of the Second World War. It was natural that sonar, which had accurately been detecting submarines below the water's surface for years, should also be used in fishing to detect underwater objects. The first flashers have since given way to paper graphs and, finally, to liquid-crystal-display readouts that actually show fish shapes on a video screen. The newest sonar units feature side scanning, which allows the angler to see in the horizontal as well as the vertical plane. Some fish finders are even equipped with games to entertain the angler when the fishing is slow.

Electric trolling motors, powered by 12-volt batteries, now enable the fisherman to maneuver almost soundlessly through shallow areas where the fish are easily frightened off. They are used with canoes as well as regular fishing boats, and are ideal for positioning or slow, silent trolling. Many models can be steered by using a foot pedal, leaving both hands free for fishing.

Other electronic developments have paved the way for further high tech additions to advanced angling equipment. Temperature gauges instantly read the surface temperature of the water, and temperature probes can be lowered into the depths to pinpoint the location of different temperature bands. There are even color meters that tell an angler which lure color works best at certain depths for clear, stained, or dirty water conditions.

AFTER A FIERCE STRUGGLE IN THE CURRENT, THIS SALMON IS FINALLY SUBDUED.

Boat designs have made a remarkable advancement in terms of speed and design. Original birchbark canoes and wooden punts have been replaced by a large variety of aluminum and fiberglass craft. Aluminum, one of the strongest and lightest of metals, is ideal for the average angler. Most fishermen have owned an aluminum boat of some kind or another, and these craft range from a simple 14-foot "cartopper" to one of the more advanced bass boats. For speed and stability on the water, fiberglass has become the premiere construction material – fiberglass boats, with their mirror-smooth hulls, are capable of speeds faster than 70 miles per hour. They enable the angler to waste little time in traveling to his hot spot. These boats come in a variety of shapes and sizes, some designed for big-water use in the Great Lakes or on the coasts where high seas are likely to occur, and others designed with super-shallow drafts so they can be maneuvered into shallow water. And, of course, all modern boats now come equipped with built-in live wells and a whole host of electronic fishing gear, making them super, high-tech fishing machines. Regardless of sophisticated equipment, some things will never change – there will always be a special place for the casually held cane pole and the dangling worm, for the peaceful relaxation and solitude of a sport that has endured over many centuries.

MODERN BASS ROATS ARE HIGH-TECH FISHING MACHINES.

Catch and Release

The terms *catch and release* and *live release* have become prominent among the ranks of today's anglers. These wise concepts are now widely practiced in all kinds of waters. They have long been practiced by the pure sportsman, usually the fly-angler. One can almost picture the first fly-fisherman laying out his delicately cast fly to tempt a wary stream trout, carefully playing the fish and then sitting back briefly to admire his catch before gently slipping it back into the water. Catch-and-release fishing is now the focus of fishing groups all across North America, which use multimedia presentations to teach proper methods and the handling of appropriate tools for the safe release of our game species. Catch and release has also become institutionalized in various game-fish laws by means of slot limits and minimum/maximum limits on the size of fish that may be kept.

A live-release angler should be properly prepared and release the catch as quickly and as safely as possible. In this chapter, we'll examine the many ways to properly release a variety of game fish, look at the tools available to aid in safe release, and cover the pros and cons of releasing the fish you catch. There are situations where catch and release is imperative and others that allow the harvesting of some fish.

A POSITIVE STEP

Catch and release is in keeping with the concern for environmental preservation and conservation. The pros and cons of the live-release solution have been discussed by top angling experts and there is no end to the debate. Many North American outdoor magazines and television programs are promoting a variant of catch and release called *selective harvest*. This philosophy allows the angler to kill some of his catch for food, yet most of the fish are released to

ensure healthy fish stocks and good angling sport in the future. Without a doubt, catch and release works. It alleviates the pressure of overfishing on fragile fish populations that would otherwise rapidly become decimated. In some cases, when larger fish are selectively released, it helps to protect the superproductive adult spawners, which are necessary in maintaining an abundant population of fish.

IMPROVING THE SUCCESS OF LIVE RELEASE

Careful, safe handling of fish to ensure a high rate of survival starts long before the fish is even landed. It begins with the selection of your gear. The choice of line strength and type of rod and bait will have a bearing on the released fish's chances for survival. The line you use, for example, will significantly influence how long you fight a fish. Use of a light line will mean a lengthy fight, which will increase the buildup of lactic acid in the fish's muscles and thus increase the stress placed on it. This result is most evident in pike and muskies that have been landed after a long struggle. Often stress from fighting causes hemorrhaging and blood drips from their fins. Fish in this condition have fewer chances of survival than fish that are fought-out quickly and then released. It should also be pointed out that river fish, already accustomed to the stress of fighting currents, are less susceptible to stress from long angling battles. A long struggle with a lake fish, however, will create real problems for its survival when it's released.

Since fishing rods and lines are usually matched according to action, the live-release angler will tend to choose slightly heavier action gear in many situations in order to shorten the fish's struggle. Light-tackle purists often criticize modern bass anglers for using 14- to 20-pound-test lines on heavyweight outfits. I would, nevertheless, rather have my fish quickly and safely landed and avoid the possibility of having it break the line on some underwater obstacle, leaving the lure stuck in its mouth. In a sense, the use of heavy line around logs and fallen trees is actually *more* sporting since it greatly improves the fish's survival chances. Fish that break light lines in heavy cover run the risk of death or injury in two ways. First, the fish may damage itself as it tries to dislodge the lure against objects. Second, the fish may die from starvation if the lure in its mouth prevents it from feeding properly.

Should the catch-and-release angler use live bait or lures? Live-bait fishermen argue that treble-hooked lures can easily damage fish and that a single bait hook is therefore better. In addition, a single hook can be left in the fish if it is too deeply hooked inside, and will often be dissolved by the fish's own fluids. Lure fishermen, in contrast, argue that the use of live bait results in more deeply hooked fish that are then fatally damaged. Both sides of the argument have merit. Live-bait anglers should always use bronze hooks that are easily dissolved by the digestive juices of the fish if the hooks cannot be removed without damaging the fish. Nickel or chrome-plated hooks dissolve much more slowly or not at all, often with fatal results. Live-bait anglers can also use quick-strike rigs that result in fewer deeply hooked fish. A simple,

VERY CAREFUL HANDLING WHEN RELEASING FISH WILL ENSURE THEIR RECOVERY AND SURVIVAL.

quick-strike rig consists of a small piece of line, ending in a hook, that is tied to the main hook as a "trailer" rig. The second hook is then attached farther down the body of the live bait so that both ends of the bait possess hooks. Thus, an instant hook set becomes possible. Although this rig may lead to fewer strikes, it will solve the problem of hooking pesky, light-biting fish that grab the "unhooked" end of the bait. It also means you don't have to wait for a fish to run with the bait and to start swallowing it before setting the hook.

Of course, barbless hooks find favor in many catch-and-release anglers' tackle boxes. It's obvious that hooks without barbs cause far less damage to fish. Some anglers also argue that their success ratio for landing fish is not compromised in the least by the use of barbless hooks. Many areas of North America have instituted laws requiring mandatory use of barbless hooks in order to protect fragile fisheries. The move toward the use of barbless hooks is gaining momentum, but still meets great resistance from anglers who fear that their catches will diminish.

SPECIAL TOOLS ARE USED TO SAFELY HANDLE FISH THAT ARE DESTINED TO BE RELEASED.

THE TOOLS OF CATCH AND RELEASE

There are a number of tools that can be used to safely handle fish that are destined to be released. Some of these tools are used only for certain species; others are useful for any fish and are a must for a catch-and-release angler.

PRECIOUS PLIERS

Needle-nose pliers are a must for every angler. A strong set of pliers will safely remove the hooks from even the toughest of fish mouths. With a good set of pliers, the angler can remove most hooks without ever actually taking the fish out of the water, which makes catch-and-release angling a breeze. And here's a word of caution – always use long-nosed pliers around big fish, especially pike and muskies. You never know when a fish is going to thrash about just as you're removing the hooks. Your fingers could also be removed if you don't use the right tool for the job.

FORCEPS, PLEASE!

Forceps or "hemostats" are a tool borrowed from the medical profession. Their clamping action allows you to quickly and safely grab the hook for removal.

They are fairly narrow and pointed so that they can be used in tight places, such as the throat of a fish. In some cases, forceps will reach farther than the heavier, bulkier pliers. Forceps are popular among river anglers because they are light enough to be pinned to the angler's vest by means of a retractor reel. However, forceps lack the rigidity and strength of pliers and are not as useful on well-hooked bigger fish like pike and muskellunge.

THE QUESTION OF NETS

Wherever possible, nets should not be used to land any species of fish. The mesh on nets, especially multistrand, polypropylene nets, can be very harmful to fish, causing split or torn fins that decrease the chances of a fish's survival. Nets can also be very abrasive, removing much of the slime coating on a fish that protects it against fungus and disease. Hooks can also get caught in the mesh and, as the fish rolls and twists, it can be severely hooked a second time.

In certain situations, such as pier fishing or on big charter boats, fish can be brought close enough for hook removal only by using a long-handled net. In these cases, the best net to use is either one with flexible rubber mesh or one with coated mesh that is gentler on the fish. Soft cotton-mesh nets are also becoming more popular.

NETS SHOULD BE USED ONLY IF NEEDED.

TAILING GLOVES: GREAT TOOLS!

The tailing glove is a recent addition to the angler's equipment and can be used for a variety of fish. The tailing of fish is most popular among stream anglers who seek salmon and trout. Most anglers grab the narrow part of the fish, just in front of the tail. This hold efficiently controls the fish for easy hook removal. Tailing gloves are a great tool to use for a variety of fish, especially big muskies and pike, and they've even been used for small sharks.

By far, the most popular tailing glove on the market is made by Normark. It is marketed as the Normark Filet Glove and was originally designed to ward off cuts from knives while an angler was filleting his catch of the day. The glove is ideal for catch-and-release fishing because it is made of a special mesh of stainless steel, nylon, and DuPont Kevlar 29. This helps prevent the protective slime coating on a fish from rubbing off. The mesh grips the fish through the slime, leaving the protective coating intact when the fish is released.

RELEASE
CRADLES ARE
THE MOST
ADVANCED
RECOVERY AND
RELEASE
SYSTEMS.

A WELCOME GAFF

You won't mind committing this gaff. Gaffs are very useful catch-and-release tools for safe handling of big pike and muskies. Contrary to popular opinion, gaffs are much safer than nets. The proper way to use a gaff is to place it in the fish's mouth and push the point down through the thin corner membrane that's found on either side of the tongue. Using this method, you avoid piercing the roof of the mouth.

THE CRADLE OF FREEDOM

The cradle is the most recent catch-and-release tool to hit the market. It's a simple affair, comprised of two long wooden poles that hold a length of soft mesh. It looks rather like a miniature version of the stretcher used by medics. To land fish with the cradle, you simply slip the device under the fish while it's still in the water and grasp the wooden frame to lift it out of the water; the fish is then supported by the mesh along the entire length of its body. Hooks can be taken out and, when the fish is to be returned to the water, it can be further supported by the cradle until it moves off on its own. Some cradles are calibrated for measurement so you can get an instant reading of the length of the fish. The catch-and-release angler can also take a quick snapshot showing the size of the fish without having to lift it from the water.

THE GRABBER

This is yet another handy tool for handling different species of fish, especially when the hooks are deep inside the mouth. This nylon/fiberglass composite tool looks similar to scissors but will lock to hold a fish's mouth open for easy access to the hooks. Simply insert the grabber into the mouth and squeeze so that the fish's mouth opens. There are no sharp points on the grabber to cut into the fish, making it a sensible addition to any angler's tackle box.

HANDLE WITH CARE!

The proper handling of fish destined to be released is perhaps the most important part of the whole catch-and-release process. It is during these moments that fish can be either quickly and safely returned to the water or doomed through irreparable damage.

Each game fish needs to be handled in its own special way. Catch and release is, after all, futile unless the fish are actually able to survive when returned to the water. Here are some of the most common game-fish species and hints on handling them.

THE PALM OF THE HAND CAN ACT JUST LIKE A RELEASE CRADLE.

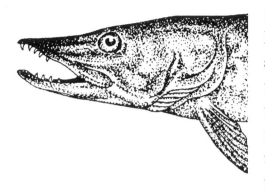

MUSKELLUNGE

Muskellunge are, perhaps, the most revered of freshwater game fish. Legend and storytelling surround this popular species and create an unequaled mystique that fascinates even the nonangler. The sheer size and fighting ability of this creature make it well worth protecting, and this view is certainly reflected in the game-fish laws designed to protect the species. Although the fight of a muskie is unforgettable, with its spectacular leaps and fierce, powerful runs, this fish should be fought out quickly, using fairly heavy tackle. An extended fight can cause hemorrhaging in the fins, leading to loss of blood.

All muskies destined for release should, if possible, be released while they are still in the water near the boat. This practice places the least stress on the fish. Often anglers will use a tape measure and camera while the fish remains in the water. Very accurate weight estimates can be made from measurements, so anglers can brag to their friends and, at the same time, be assured that their muskie has an excellent chance of surviving to breed. If the hooks are imbedded deeply in the mouth or throat of a muskie and it has to be brought into the boat or onto shore, then the safest method of handling the fish is to use a cradling device. If a cradle isn't available, then the fish should be supported by holding it below the jaw (but not in the gills) with one hand and partway down the body with the other hand. With this handling technique the angler must constantly guard against dropping the fish if it suddenly starts to thrash! Yanking a fish out of the water with its whole weight supported by the jaw can be very detrimental, especially to big fish. The weight of a big fish can stretch its spine and also cause tearing in the body cavity when the internal organs are allowed to sag in an unnatural position.

Although it may sound contradictory, the use of a gaff is often recommended for big muskies. A gaff will actually cause less damage than a net, which can slice fins and scrape off scales. When used properly, a gaff causes no life-threatening damage to the fish. The gaff point should be inserted into the thin tissue in the crook of the mouth and nowhere else.

If a muskie must be brought into the boat, the hooks should be removed with all possible speed so the fish can be returned quickly to the water. Simply removing the hooks as fast as possible, however, is only half the battle. The process of releasing the fish safely often takes longer than the fighting and landing of the fish. A muskie should always be gently cradled with both hands until it can swim away. If you have to use your hands, firmly grip its caudle peduncle (the narrow section just in front of the tail) and place your other hand under its belly, holding the fish upright under the surface of the water. If the muskie has undergone severe stress, then a forward figure-eight motion will help wash fresh, oxygenated water over its gills. Never pull the fish backwards in the water because this may cause fatal damage to its gills. Once the fish is struggling on its own to get away, then it can simply be released. Be sure, however, to watch for signs that the fish has not fully recovered. It's not uncommon to see a fish swim several feet away, only to resurface lying on its side. The revival process must then be repeated patiently.

NORTHERN PIKE

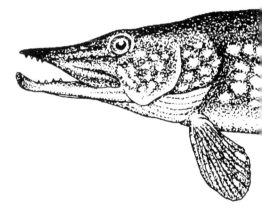

Large northern pike should be handled like the muskellunge. Smaller pike and muskies, however, can often be handled in a much simpler way. The safest way to release all species is by removing the hooks as the fish rest horizontally in the water. Keeping them in their own environment avoids the great stress of bringing them into the air, which is as uncomfortable to an exhausted fish as water is to humans. If necessary, however, small pike and muskies can be gripped firmly at the side of the head where the gill plates meet the body. *Never, never, never* grip the fish by placing your fingers into its eye cavities, as has so horribly been the custom in years gone by. This practice can quite easily kill the fish by permanently impairing its vision. Once small pike have been landed, they can be held vertically for a short period of time in order to remove the hooks. If hook removal has been particularly difficult, then the fish may require resuscitation under the water's surface until it regains enough energy to move away on its own.

LARGEMOUTH AND SMALLMOUTH BASS

Largemouth and smallmouth bass can be easily held by the mouth because their teeth are very small. Yes, they do have teeth, hundreds of them in fact, but they're so tiny that they're almost unnoticeable when the angler grabs the fish by the lower jaw. Under a microscope, the many teeth of a bass look like something out of a horror movie. Because they are so short and tightly grouped together, they feel much less fearsome – almost like a man's two-day growth of beard. The best way to successfully catch and release bass is by playing them out quickly. They should then be "lipped" by firmly gripping their lower jaw between thumb and forefinger so they can be hoisted up to remove the hooks. Some anglers grip small bass by placing a hand around their mid-section, but this method is not recommended. Not only does it remove some of the disease-preventing slime from their bodies, but it can also damage internal organs if excessive pressure is applied.

When bass are caught with crankbaits, placing fingers in the same jaw that contains an array of sharp treble hooks can be tricky. One head shake from a spunky fish can lead to some nasty consequences. In this situation it's best to remove the hooks with needle-nose pliers as the fish rests in the water.

Most bass are hardy fish that can be played out, then easily slipped back into the water after the hooks have been removed. The need for gentle handing cannot be overemphasized. It takes only a few seconds to lean over and gently slip the fish into the water. There's no need to unceremoniously throw a fish back into the water. A carelessly tossed fish is easily damaged by the impact with the water's surface and, even if it swims away, it may die later from its injuries.

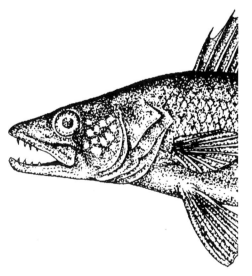

WALLEYE

Like bass, walleye are hardy fish. Unlike bass, they cannot be handled by the lower jaw. The frightening array of teeth in the mouth of a walleye make "lipping" it impossible. If the fish must be lifted because it can't be unhooked in the water, a firm and sure grip at the back of the gill plates usually does the job. If large walleye are picked up, they should be cradled with one hand under the belly while the other grips the tail. Such handling supports the fish to prevent spinal and other internal damage. Again, care must be taken against dropping the fish if it struggles. Often, releasing this species involves only a moment of gently holding the fish in the water until it slips away on its own.

TROUT AND SALMON IN SHALLOW WATER

Atlantic, chinook, and coho salmons, along with rainbow, brown, and brook trouts, can be handled in much the same way prior to release. Stream fish are best landed as quickly as possible – the longer you fight a fish, the longer the revival process will likely take. For the stream angler, there are many methods of landing fish, such as "beaching" the fish onto shore (not recommended for live-release fish) or guiding it into extremely shallow water (excellent choice), netting, and tailing it with a special glove. By far the best way to successfully release a stream-caught fish is to take the hook out with a quick tug as the fish lies in the water. Using barbless hooks makes this even easier because they require no tug, just a simple gentle pull – no damage, no fuss.

When returning a fish to its stream, face it in an upstream direction so that fresh, oxygenated water flows over its gills. When it fights to free itself from your grasp, you know it's strong enough to swim away on its own.

DEEP-WATER FISH SPECIES

Deep-water fish species, such as salmon and, especially, lake trout, offer unique catch-and-release difficulties. When deep-water fish are suddenly brought to the surface, often their air bladder expands greatly as a result of the rapid decrease in atmospheric pressure. In some cases the air-bladder swelling is so great that it is actually forced out of the fish's mouth. The principle of fighting a fish quickly to prevent toxic lactic acid buildup should therefore be ignored for these deep-water fish. There are a few ways to cope with this problem and increase the chances of a successful live release. The first thing to do is to fight the fish *slowly* so that it has a chance to compensate for the decreased atmospheric pressure as it moves toward the surface. If a fish has a visibly bulging air bladder when it is landed, it can be "burped" by running a hand along its sides from the mid-lateral region forward toward the head. By this means you can release the trapped air, allowing the fish to maintain its equilibrium once it is returned to the water. Another method of handling a fish with an enlarged air bladder is to puncture the bladder with a needle, thereby allowing the excess air to escape.

When releasing fish that have been landed from deep water, take the time to make sure that they can swim away on their own. Watch the water for some time afterward to see if the injured fish floats back up to the surface. If this happens and the fish cannot be revived, then retrieve it and have it for dinner.

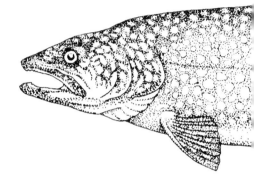

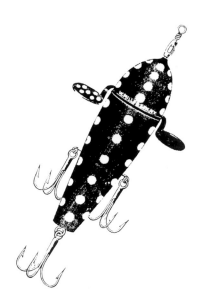

THE CATCH-AND-RELEASE DEBATE

The philosophical debate surrounding the practice of catch-and-release continues. Picture this scenario. Mr. Joseph Pro has recently purchased a fancy, supercharged bass boat. He has acquired all of the latest technology, including 100 percent graphite rods: the lightest, strongest, and most sensitive models that money can buy. His formidable craft is bedecked with all the electronics imaginable and, of course, he has an electric motor for precise positioning and pinpoint casting. Next to him is Mr. Jonathan Doe, an average type of angler, in a 14-foot aluminum boat with no fancy electronics, just a plain 10-horsepower engine, a pair of oars, and a few trusty old lures. Mr. Pro knows the game well and reels in bass after bass. He powers the fish to the boat, then quickly and expertly flips them back into the water with a loud splash, releasing more than thirty fish in all. Mr. Doe catches a few fish, three to be exact, and puts them on a stringer for the table before leaving with a satisfied expression on his face. Mr. Pro is horrified. How can anyone keep a fish as revered as the bass for the table – it's sacrilege. He moves off, snorting in disgust.

So, who is the conservationist in this situation? Well, it's certainly *not* the pro – he's probably killed countless fish with his careless release tactics. Studies concerning delayed mortality rates among bass suggest that perhaps 20 percent of the pro's "flapjacked" fish were injured enough to die later. That means that the *ill-informed* catch-and-release angler managed to kill and waste five fish compared to only three by the catch-and-keep (and eat) angler.

This small anecdote illustrates the need to examine the catch-and-release issue from all of its different perspectives. It is, after all, very easy to "jump on the band wagon" and stubbornly declare that live releasing is the correct procedure in *every* case when tolerance is called for instead.

Whether you catch and release all of the fish you catch or keep a reasonable few as a limited harvest, it's important to remember every fish released today helps to ensure a healthy fish population for the future.

THE FUTURE LIES
IN OUR HANDS.

Arctic Char

J. REIST

FEW GAME FISH
ARE AS BRIGHTLY
COLORED AS A
CHAR PRIOR TO
SPAWNING.

COMMON NAMES alpine char, Arctic char, Arctic salmon, blueback trout, Coppermine River salmon, ekaluk, European char, Greenland char, Hearne's salmon, Hudson Bay salmon, ivitaruk, Quebec red trout, sea trout

DESCRIPTION This char has a trout-like body with a deeply forked tail. The head is relatively short, and the males may develop a protrusion or kype on the lower jaw. Arctic char are best known for their splendid colors, although nonspawning adults may be only plain silver. A char in full spawning array, however, is a magnificent sight to behold. The upper body may appear dark or bluish green. The sides are often silvery, sometimes with a blue tinge, and are adorned with pink or red spots. Occasionally, the sides may even turn flaming orange. The belly colors range from orange to red, and the leading edges of the pectoral and pelvic fins are white.

SIZE In general, Arctic char grow slowly and reach their full size at twenty years. The average sea-run char weighs between 2 and 10 pounds. Fish of 15 and 20 pounds, however, are reported each year by anglers, which makes the current world record all the more interesting. This record fish was caught on July 30, 1981, in the Tree River in Canada. It was a colossus, weighing 32 pounds, 9 ounces.

DISTRIBUTION Arctic char are appropriately named, for they have the most northerly distribution of any freshwater fish. They are found in lakes and rivers throughout the northern hemisphere, including North America, Asia, Europe,

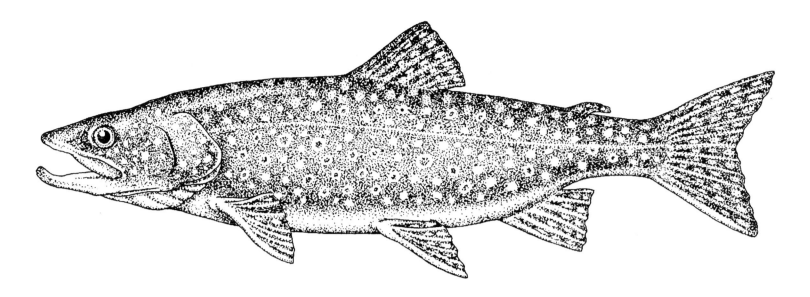

Iceland, and Greenland. In Canada this char occurs in Newfoundland, Labrador, and eastern Quebec, and across the northern coastline, including the various Arctic islands. The U.S. range of the Arctic char is restricted to Alaska.

BEHAVIOR AND HABITAT Char spawn sometime between September and October on gravel or rock shoals in lakes and in slow pools in rivers. Spawning depths may vary from 3 to 15 feet, and a redd or nest is prepared by the female who uses her tailfin in a sweeping motion along the bottom of the river or lake. A female may deposit some 3,000 to 5,000 eggs, which are fertilized by the attendant male as they are laid. Females are able to spawn only every second or third year. The eggs are covered in the bottom gravel and hatch the following year, between April and July. During the same summer, the fry leave the river and return to the sea, although some populations remain permanently in fresh water. Studies have revealed the amazingly varied dietary habits of this char. They are, of

course, carnivorous, and a large range of fish have been found in their stomachs, including sculpins, lumpfishes, seasnails, Arctic cod, sand lance, and other Arctic char. In fresh water, char gobble up insect larvae, clams, smelt, sticklebacks, brook trout, and even other char. Cannibalism of young fish by the

Arctic char in rivers are often concentrated behind boulders and other obstacles that break the flow of the current. Although these areas are fairly easy to recognize, they are not quite as easy to fish. When the current is especially fast, it's important to cast the lures well upstream, allowing them to sink to the depth of the fish before retrieving them past the fish when the current brings them near the "strike zone." Brightly colored lines can be employed to better track the tumultuous movement of the line in the heavy currents. A "stop and go" retrieve can also help to stir up inactive char.

larger adults, together with predation by loons and terns, are the only natural dangers to this species.

FISHING TACKLE Arctic char are pursued by the fly-fisherman and the spin-fisherman alike. The type of fly gear is dependent on the kind of water being fished. In general, the same types of outfits used by steelheaders can also be employed for Arctic char. For small fish, 5-weight outfits are fine, whereas large char in fast waters require 7- to 9-weight rods. The spin-fisherman, too, should build his outfit around the anticipated size of the fish and the nature of the water. A good ultra-light outfit can provide sport and pleasure for the smaller fish, while a 7-foot, medium-action rod and reel may be needed for large char.

FISHING TECHNIQUES Fly-fishermen, plying the coastal haunts of the char, usually cast forage fish or shrimp imitations. When the char move upriver, however, a whole range of flies become effective, including wet and dry flies, egg imitations, and streamers. Dry-fly patterns are used mainly where there is great insect activity, such as during large caddis-fly hatches. Most anglers rely more heavily on wet flies, and often the same patterns that are used for steelhead will be effective for char as well. Bright colors, slow retrieves, and the occasional twitch is the secret of fly-fishing success for char. Some favorite flies are the Teal and Yellow, the Bloody Butcher, the Blue Zulu, the Teal and Green, and the Mallard and Claret.

Spin-fishermen usually use various types of real or imitation egg baits. A variety of brightly colored spinners and spoons are also effective.

OPPOSITE:

CHAR —

MEMORIES IN

VIVID COLOR.

Arctic Grayling

COMMON NAMES American grayling, Arctic grayling, Arctic trout, Back's grayling, bluefish, grayling, sailfin arctic grayling, tittimeg

DESCRIPTION Arctic grayling hold a special mystique for many southern anglers. Their pronounced dorsal fin, richly imbued with colorful spots, makes them one of the most unusual and handsome fish in North America. Grayling hit hard, make good runs, and often leap repeatedly when hooked, making them a sort of rainbow trout of the north. Grayling are also evocative of wilderness angling and fast-paced action, giving them a reputation rivaled by few other fish in North America.

Male and female grayling are strikingly colored; both are silvery gray, with a purple to blue iridescence. The sides are marked with numerous V-shaped or diamond-shaped spots. The head is olive-green with a mauve iridescence, and mauve bands also border the dorsal fin. Mauve and orange areas run down the prominent pelvic fins. Females are usually less brightly colored than males, and tend to have shorter dorsal fins; the depressed dorsals of males extend back to or beyond the adipose fin.

SIZE The size of grayling varies almost predictably according to fishing pressure. In heavily fished populations along such areas as the Alaska Highway, a 12-inch fish may be considered large because many of the larger fish were caught years ago. A 5-pound, 15-ounce fish was caught in 1967 on the Katseyedie River, N.W.T. Today, a 20-inch fish

THE MALES HAVE AN EVEN LARGER DORSAL FIN THAN THE FEMALES.

CRAIG ORR

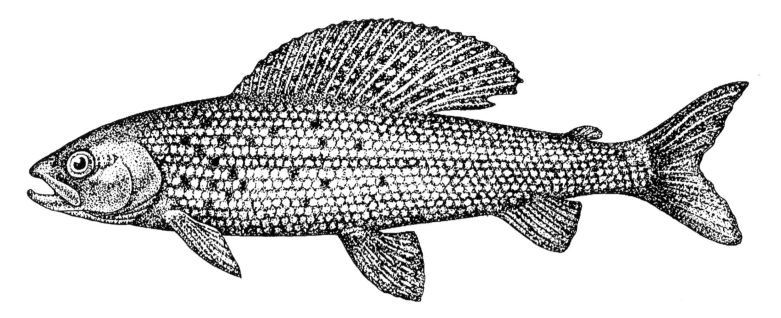

of about 2.5 to 3 pounds is considered a trophy. Grayling of that size are usually found only in wilderness areas of Alaska, the Yukon, parts of the northern Prairie provinces, and in the Northwest Territories. Fish of this size have also recently come out of northern British Columbia in newly opened fisheries near Tootsie and Nome lakes, operated by Kawdy Outfitters.

DISTRIBUTION The Arctic grayling occurs in northern freshwater drainages of North America, Europe, and Asia. In Canada, grayling are found from the western drainages of Hudson Bay west to Alaska, including northern Saskatchewan, Manitoba, Alberta, and British Columbia. A population of grayling once existed in rivers flowing into lakes Michigan, Huron, and Superior in northern Michigan. Perhaps the most famous of these rivers was Michigan's Au Sable, where grayling were wiped out during an era of unregulated logging and relentless angling. Grayling are still found in the headwaters of the Missouri River above Great Falls, Montana, and they

have been introduced into the mountainous areas of such states as Vermont, Utah, and Colorado.

BEHAVIOR AND HABITAT Grayling feed almost entirely on aquatic and terrestrial insects, including mayflies, caddis flies, bees, wasps,

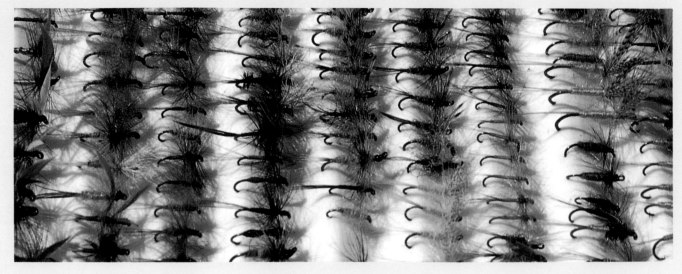

1 Since grayling love dry flies, make sure your offerings are as good as they can be. Dry flies often become quite scrawny-looking after a lot of use, and fly anglers often discard them. This is unnecessary. All you have to do to make them appealing to grayling is to steam them over a pot of boiling water. For those flies that won't respond even to this treatment, just trim off the bedraggled hackles and feathers and form them into "no name" nymphs. They really work!

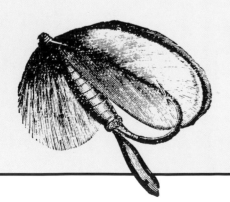

2 If the grayling are hitting near the surface on wet flies, here's a tip to make your fly stay near the surface better. Just tie a second knot, such as the Portland Creek Half Hitch on the fly. This will ensure that it rides in the surface film in a manner irresistible to the grayling.

3 When grayling are less than eager to hit your spinner, try slowing down your presentation. Cast across the stream at right angles to the current. Retrieve slowly enough to allow the current to carry your lure in a slow, tantalizing arc across the tail of the pool.

4 Small spoons are very effective lures when the grayling are resting behind rocks or other current breaks. Stand above the rock or obstruction and cast just upstream from it. Allow the spoon to hang in the current for a moment and then let it flutter down current past the hiding fish before tightening the line again. The lure will hover near the fish, drawing strikes where other lures will fail.

5 One of the misconceptions about grayling is that they have mouths of soft tissue. This leads some anglers to set the hook half-heartedly to avoid losing fish. Unfortunately, the fish ends up being lightly hooked and lost anyway. To set the record straight, grayling have small but leathery mouths. The hook should be set with a short but firm jerk of the wrist. While playing the fish, maintain steady pressure, keeping the line tight.

grasshoppers, ants, beetles, and midges. Grayling will also eat small fish whenever these are available.

Grayling are a "sit and wait" predator in streams. They station themselves close to the middle of streams until prey drift toward them on the current. Often they congregate at the base of waterfalls or other sites where food is most concentrated. They feed on drifting objects in and on the surface of the water.

The general habitat of grayling is the clear water of medium to large, cold rivers, though they are also found in lakes, often near stream mouths and in shallow bays during the summer.

FISHING TACKLE Because of their varied diet, and the low angling pressure characteristic of wilderness fishing, grayling are obligingly unselective when it comes to fishing tackle. They will take live bait, but it is usually not necessary, since grayling will readily pursue a wide variety of spinners. Small spoons may also be a good choice. Copper and silver are favorite color selections.

An ultra-light spinning outfit of 5 to 6 feet in length is a good choice.

The wilderness habitat of the grayling also makes it an outstanding fish for fly-casters. Any small insect-like pattern will probably attract fish. A No. 8 or smaller hook is recommended, and fly color is not too important. Grayling are excellent targets for both dry and sinking flies. A 3- or 5-weight rod is recommended.

FISHING TECHNIQUES Grayling are likely to be concentrated near river mouths, below waterfalls, and in shallow bays of lakes. They can often be spotted cruising in the clear waters of such areas, feeding on or just under the surface. To catch a surface-feeding fish, a surface fly should be used first, before proceeding to a wet fly, or even a spinner. Grayling often hit hard on the retrieve, so a series of short retrieves should be employed. Long casts are not generally needed on many grayling streams.

Atlantic Salmon

OUANANICHE CLOSELY RESEMBLES THE BROWN TROUT.

COMMON NAMES Atlantic salmon, black salmon, common Atlantic salmon, grilse, kelt, Kennebec salmon, Lake Atlantic salmon, landlocked salmon, ouananiche, sebago, sebago salmon

DESCRIPTION The Atlantic salmon is undoubtedly the aristocrat of North American game fish. Indeed, it has traditionally been pursued by wealthy anglers who can afford to travel to the often remote locations where this salmon still thrives. The Atlantic has a long, slender body, much like a trout. During spawning runs, the males develop a hooked jaw or "kype." The tail is only slightly forked and the scales are relatively large. At sea, the Atlantic sports bright silver sides marked by only a sparse series of X-shaped, black spots. The back is usually black, brown, or blue, and the belly is silvery to white in color. After these salmon have entered spawning rivers, they gradually turn a bronze and dark brown. Sometimes they also develop red spots on their heads and bodies. They are usually darkest in color after they have spawned, and are then often referred to as "black." The landlocked version of the Atlantic is called "ouananiche." It is believed that landlocked salmon were first trapped in freshwater lakes millennia ago when changes in the earth's crust cut spawning Atlantic salmon off from the sea.

SIZE Anadromous or migratory Atlantics may return to spawning rivers after only one year as "grilse,"

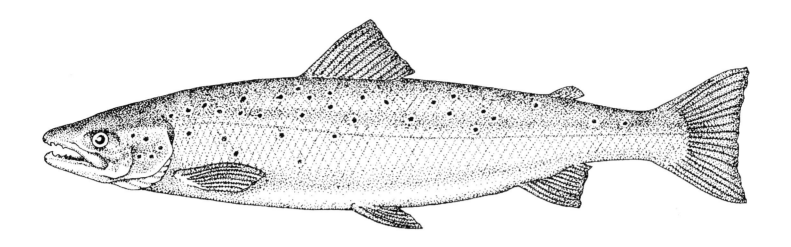

weighing about 4 or 5 pounds. Those fish that return after two years often weigh between 7 and 15 pounds, although the world-record fish, caught in Norway in 1928, weighed more than 79 pounds. Landlocked salmon or ouananiche are usually smaller, weighing between 2 and 4 pounds on average. Large fish of more than 35 and of 44 pounds have been caught in Sebago Lake, Maine, and in Lake Ontario, Canada, respectively.

DISTRIBUTION Atlantic salmon are found in all areas adjacent to the North Atlantic Ocean. In the U.S., Atlantic salmon are found in the uppermost northeastern states. In Canada they are in Newfoundland, Labrador and the Maritimes, and in parts of eastern and northern Quebec. Although a population of nonmigratory Atlantics used to flourish in Lake Ontario, they disappeared in the late 1800s and that species has only recently been reintroduced. In fact, most stocking programs have not been successful, although salmon plantings in 1935 in Trout Lake near North Bay have

succeeded in creating a naturally reproducing population.

BEHAVIOR AND HABITAT Immature Atlantics spend two to three years in fresh water before migrating to sea. They return after one or two years to spawn in their native

rivers, usually during October and November. Landlocked salmon spawning behavior is similar to that of migratory Atlantics except that ouananiche move from lake to river. Females choose the nesting site, which often consists of a gravel bed above or below a pool. The nest is dug by the female vigorously thrashing her tail over the spawning gravel. A 20-pound female may release up to 14,000 eggs, which are covered with gravel by the movements of the female's tail. The spawned-out fish, known as "kelts," may remain in the river for a number of weeks before returning to the sea or lake. Atlantic salmon do not all die after spawning, as do the Pacific salmon. At sea, Atlantics will feed on a wide variety of marine creatures, including crustaceans and fish such as rainbow smelt, alewives, Atlantic herring, capelin, and small Atlantic cod or Atlantic mackerel. During their spawning phase, they will not feed, and it is not known exactly why they willingly take the angler's lures. Ouananiche usually remain in shallow lake waters immediately after spawning and fall back into deeper water as the summer arrives. In the fall they will again enter the shallow water and commence their spawning cycle once more.

S P E C I A L   T I P

The Atlantic-salmon angler must learn to spot the areas or lies that salmon like. There are a few tricks that will help. First, invest in a good pair of polarized sunglasses so you can spot the rises and other signs of salmon activity. Look for basketball-sized rocks that create a "V" in the current. Salmon also like to lie directly alongside very large boulders that are found in rushing currents. Trough-shaped pools as well as crotches of forks in rivers are favorite taking lies.

The outside edges of river bends and pools with shale ledges have also proved successful. Atlantics generally prefer the shallow tails of pools. Remember that, once discovered, a salmon lie will likely be productive year after year.

FISHING TACKLE Bait-fish imitations are most effective in spring when the salmon are feeding in the shallows. In the fall, attractor patterns are more effective since ouananiche are less inclined to feed. Where it is permitted, the spin-fisherman can either cast or troll for ouananiche with medium-action rods and reels. Favorite lures, fished with 8-pound-test line, are often those that best imitate bait fish. The Moose-Look Wobbler in silver, brass, copper, and orange; the Flash-King in red-gold or blue-silver; and the Blue Fox Pixie in pink-silver and white-silver are all popular bait-fish lures. Trollers also use smelt or shiners for bait trolling, especially after ice-out. Even the fly-fisherman employs trolling techniques, using large single or tandem streamer flies tied on 4X long or 6X long hooks. Popular streamer and bucktail patterns include the Grey Ghost, Black Ghost, Barnes Special, Pink Lady, and Mickey Finn.

FISHING TECHNIQUES Atlantics, whether landlocked ouananiche or sea-run, are spectacular fighters, especially in the river habitat, which is traditionally the domain of the Atlantic salmon fly-fisherman. The fly-fisher usually uses 8 1/2- to 9-foot rods with reels capable of holding approximately 150 yards of

backing as well as a complete fly line. Leaders are often made of 6- to 12-pound test line and are sometimes 9 to 12 feet long.

During the summer when waters are lower and clearer, fly leaders should be scaled down to 3- or 5-pound test. Similarly, summertime dry flies are also much smaller, often tied on a No. 6, 8, or 10 hook. Locating Atlantics can be a daunting task. Atlantic salmon are usually not found in river locales that attract trout. Often they will be found in some very improbable locations, such as any relatively shallow stretch of the spawning river. The angler also has the problem of distinguishing between temporary holding lies and feeding lies. Most of the time, depths of 3 or 4 feet are preferred, and fish seem to return to the same lies year after year—a fact that is not lost on experienced Atlantic-salmon anglers.

It is suspected that nonfeeding salmon strike flies for a variety of reasons. It could be instinctive aggression, territoriality, or memories of feeding on insects as a parr. Whatever the reason, the fly must be presented correctly. For wet flies, a broadside presentation across the lie is generally preferred over a downstream drift.

Dry fly-fishing is often conducted under very clear weather and water conditions in summer, and Atlantics do take drys eagerly at times. In this fishing style, the flies are cast across and slightly downstream. Ouananiche, unlike trout, are unpredictable and may require innumerable repeat casts before they suddenly strike. The angler normally wears sunglasses and looks for salmon or boiling water from moving fish. The lie is then methodically and thoroughly covered until the fish is coaxed into striking. The strike is not at all like that of a trout, which will quickly drop the angler's offering unless the hook is set very quickly. The ouananiche angler needs to allow the fish a little time to actually get the fly in its mouth before setting the hook.

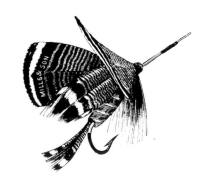

1 Atlantics like to take a fly that appears to be suspended over them. When you identify a feeding lie, cast the fly so that it swings across the current and over the fish. Always suspend the fly in the current over the fish for a few moments before retrieving it for another cast.

2 Make sure your flies are presented to the salmon in a "broadside" manner. Atlantics can be very finicky takers and will usually ignore flies that they cannot see silhouetted entirely.

3 Nobody knows exactly why Atlantic salmon hit flies. Atlantics are unpredictable and may strike a fly at any time. For this reason, make sure you cast to an Atlantic in a persistent manner. Casts should be made to a visible fish about twenty or thirty times. If the fish doesn't seem interested, don't give up too quickly!

4 Atlantic salmon are renowned the world over for their excellent fighting qualities. Fly-fishermen often use extension butts that pop into the bottom of their fly rods. These "fighting" butts give the angler much more leverage during the fight and are particularly useful for battling salmon in fast water.

5 Many fly-anglers also troll flies for ouananiche. Two basic streamer flies are tied to a full sinking line: single and tandem. The tandem streamers are made by attaching two long shank hooks together with a short piece of monofilament line. These tandem designs are easy to tie and have the advantage of tracking through the water easily and increasing hook-setting ability.

Brook Trout

SCOTT RIPLEY

LARGE BROOKIES THAT ARE RELEASED WILL PROVIDE BROOD STOCK FOR TOMORROW'S FISHERY.

COMMON NAMES aurora trout, breac, brookie, brook trout, coaster, eastern speckled trout, mountain trout, mud trout, native trout, sea trout, speckled char, speckled trout, square-tail, squaretailed trout

DESCRIPTION The brook trout is native to North America and much admired for its delicate beauty. It is a member of the *Salmonidae* family along with salmons, trouts, chars, whitefishes, and graylings. It has an elongated, typically trout-like shape with a fairly large head. The tail or caudal fin is only slightly forked, hence the name "square-tail." The remarkably beautiful color patterns of the brookie are reminiscent of more tropical climes. The brookie's back is an olive green or brown and is graced with a complex network of worm-like lines called "vermiculations" that serve as camouflage. Along its sides this char is usually yellow-green or orange, and the belly is often white. The sides of the brookie are adorned with many spots, including a smattering of small red dots surrounded by stunning pale-blue halos or "aureoles." The ventral fins are often orange to red, with a white and then a black line along their leading edges. The brookie has been hybridized with the lake trout to produce the "splake," which often looks much like brook trout. Brook trout have also been crossed with brown trout to produce tiger trout whose suggestive side markings have given the

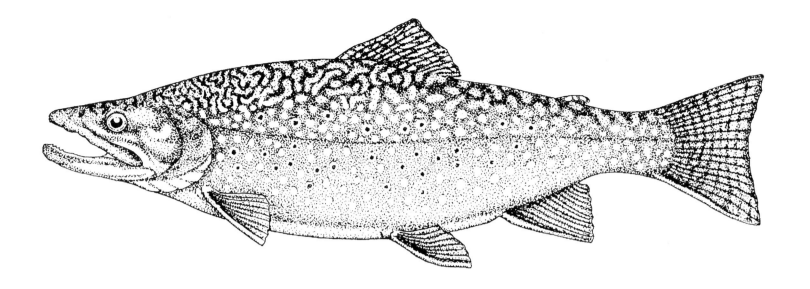

hybrid its name. Brookies have even been artificially crossed with kokanee salmon.

SIZE The typical stream brookie is not known for its great size and usually measures 8 to 12 inches in length and weighs less than a pound. In the lake habitat, however, these fish can grow much larger and commonly attain weights of several pounds. A trophy lake specimen would weigh between 5 and 7 pounds. Brookies are also sea-run and, although these fish attain larger "average" sizes, they seldom produce the trophy-sized lunkers of their freshwater cousins. Wild brookies seldom live longer than five years, although one wonders how old the world-record fish might have been. This 14-pound, 8-ounce lunker was caught in the Nipigon River of Ontario, Canada, in 1916.

DISTRIBUTION The brook trout is found throughout the Maritimes, Newfoundland, and Labrador. It is common in Quebec and Ontario and is found in the northeastern corner of Manitoba. In the United

States the brook trout occurs in the northeastern states, in the Appalachian Mountains south to Georgia, in the upper Mississippi and in the Great Lakes drainage areas of Minnesota. It has been widely introduced in river systems in the west.

SPECIAL TIP

Brookies can often be enticed with small natural baits, even on days when they will hit nothing else. This technique requires light lines and tiny hooks, often as small as No. 14, 16, or 18, which enable the angler to use extremely small and subtle baits that can be drifted to the inactive brookies. Often a 24-inch leader of even thinner line, perhaps 2-pound test, is used. There is no difficulty in finding baits for these sneaky rigs either. Many of the aquatic fly species have larvae that can be easily found under stream rocks, including the stonefly, caddis fly, dragonfly, and mayfly. Other easily found baits include grasshoppers, various grubs, and, of course, worms, although much smaller than the nightcrawler variety. Try it – a light line, a small hook, and a tiny something wriggling enticingly.

BEHAVIOR AND HABITAT Brook-trout spawning occurs in late summer or autumn, depending on latitude and water temperature. The most common months are September through December. The actual spawning site is carefully chosen. In streams, brookies seek out cold, spring-fed waters with gravel bottoms. In lakes, brookies will spawn in the shallows over bark, twigs, or other bottom material. The female fans a "redd" or nest with her tail and lays numerous eggs, which are fertilized with clouds of milt from the accompanying male. Numbers of eggs vary with the size of the female, but a 14-inch fish may lay 1,200 eggs. Eggs hatch according to temperature. In a temperature of 55 degrees Fahrenheit, for example, incubation would take no longer than thirty-five days. Brookies require cold water—a temperature of more than 77 degrees Fahrenheit is lethal. The preferred temperature range is between 57 and 60 degrees Fahrenheit. Although they have good tolerance to both acid and alkaline waters, they are less hardy and adaptable to extreme environmental changes than either the brown or the rainbow trout. They are also the easiest of the trouts or chars to catch, and overfishing has definitely contributed to a decline in their distribution.

Brookies are carnivorous and feed on almost anything that moves. Worms, leeches, crustaceans, mayflies, caddis flies, blackflies, spiders, and snails are all readily devoured. Other fish, such as minnows, sticklebacks, and even young trout, are also included in this voracious char's diet.

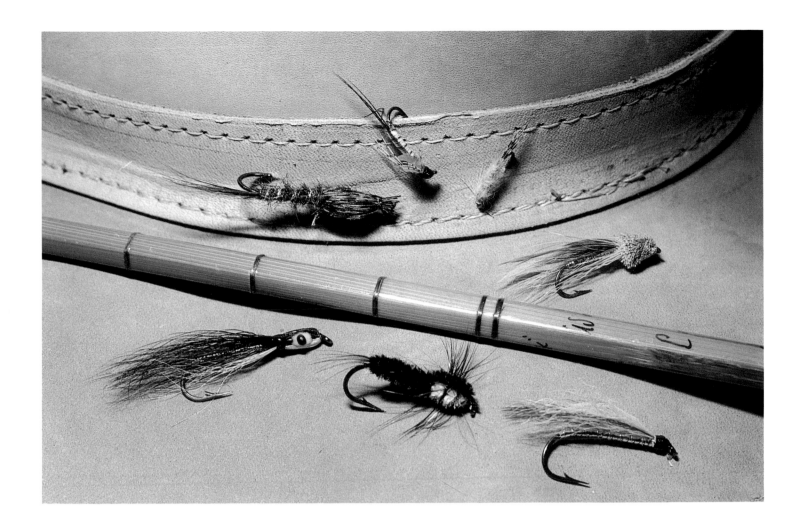

FISHING TACKLE The fly-fisherman, troller, bait-angler, and spin-fisherman all enjoy good sport with brook trout. On small streams, light outfits with light lines of 4- to 6-pound test are commonly preferred since the fish are usually small. For larger fish, medium-action spinning rods with 6- to 8-pound-test lines are used, whereas fly-fishermen resort to 9-foot rods with 6-to 7-pound-test leaders. Most small spinning lures from the spinner, spoon, or plug groups will work in the many streams, small beaver ponds, and lakes that are inhabited by speckies. The various Mepps and Blue Fox spinners are universal favorites. Among the spoons the redoubtable

E.G.B. is considered to be the number-one lure; however, small floating Rapalas and other minnow-like plugs are also increasingly popular. Fly-fishermen constantly experiment with new or different patterns of flies, streamers, and nymphs. Subsurface favorites include the Royal Coachman, the Professor, and the Gray Hackle. First among streamers are the Mickey Finn, the Green Ghost, and the White Marabou. Dry-fly fanatics often use the Hendrickson, the Cream Variant, or the Quilt Gordon. Most fly-fishers attempt to choose the fly that most matches the insect that is hatching on the day they are fishing.

A FLY WILL OUTPRODUCE SPINNING LURES HANDS DOWN.

1 Here's a good way to catch the most natural possible bait for stream brookies. Attach a square piece of screen or nylon mesh to two pieces of strapping. Hold this in the water and walk slowly upstream, moving stones and debris with your boots. You'll be surprised at the different types of bait that you capture in the screen. So will the brook trout.

2 Is there a good fish in the pool or not? To find out, just catch a grasshopper and remove one leg before tossing it upstream from the pool. If there's a feeding trout around it will not pass up this free meal. Now's the time to give it your all with your favorite fly, bait, or lure.

3 Stream brookies are wary, so it's important to walk only upstream to all of your favorite pools. Walk quietly and try to present a low profile, which is much harder for the fish to pick up. Some anglers even resort to camouflage clothing.

4 Always wear a good pair of polarized sunglasses for your stream fishing. Not only will you be able to spot the brookie moving about or rising to take a bug, but you'll be able to discern underwater structure that might conceal fish.

5 If brookies are constantly biting off the lower half of your worm, you can use a "stinger." Just attach a worm-sized length of 2- to 4-pound-test line to your hook and tie on a second, preferably smaller hook. Thread the worm over both hooks so that one is near the top and the second near the bottom. Now invite that short-striking brookie to try again.

FISHING TECHNIQUES Small streams offer a fascinating opportunity for the spin-fisherman as well as the sophisticated fly-angler. The cardinal rule is "stream craft" and this means stealth tactics. Pools and runs should be approached with the utmost caution and patience. The spin-fisherman casts his small spinners and spoons to various obstructions and cover in the various pools. Ideally, ultra-light rods and reels are used to achieve casting precision. For the fly-angler, the tangles of alder, dogwood, and overhanging cedar make fly-casting a true challenge, so the roll cast and the "dangle" are often employed. Because of heavy obstructions, wet flies are often fished down and across the stream. Lake fishermen usually troll for the much larger brookies that are found in these larger bodies of water. Often one angler steers the boat and runs a trolling line at mid-depths along the shoreline of a lake while the other casts small spinners and spoons to the more shallow water near shore. This team approach enables trollers to quickly discover the fishes' movement patterns for that day.

Brown Trout

COMMON NAMES breac, brown trout, brownie, English brown trout, European brown trout, gealag, German, German brown trout, German trout, Loch Leven trout, truite, von Behr trout

DESCRIPTION The brown trout has the characteristic long, sleek trout body and a nonforked tail. It possesses a large mouth, which, in the male, becomes extremely hooked at times, almost to the point of deformity. Although color patterns vary somewhat with different populations, this trout is generally brown or greenish on the back, fading to a creamy brown on the sides, and has a white or yellowish belly. In stream-dwelling populations, the characteristic black spots on the side of the fish are complemented with red dots. In lakes and at sea, browns are a uniform bright silver.

SIZE Brown trout can reach great sizes, especially in lake or sea-run populations. In the Great Lakes, for example, fish of 20 to 30 pounds have been taken, and specimens weighing 10 or more pounds are caught

regularly. Native browns in streams and rivers often weigh between 1 and 2 pounds, and catches weighing more than 5 pounds are considered true trophies. The International Game Fish Association lists the all-tackle record brown trout as 39

BROWN TROUT NEVER GIVE UP WITHOUT A FIGHT!

SCOTT RIPLEY

STREAM BROWNS
LOVE TO HOLD IN
POOLS WITH
STRUCTURE.

pounds, 15 ounces. It was caught by some happy angler in Nahuel Huapi, Argentina, in 1952.

DISTRIBUTION This trout is native to Europe, from the Mediterranean to the Black Sea, including Scandinavia and even Siberia. It was introduced into North America in 1883 with brown-trout eggs from Germany and later with strains imported from Loch Leven in Scotland. Since then the brown has become firmly established in many North American waters. In the United States, flourishing populations exist on the east coast as well as the western half of the country. In Canada, brown trout are abundant in southern Ontario and Quebec, as well as in southern Alberta. Extensive stocking has produced a spectacular lake-run fishery in the Great Lakes.

BEHAVIOR AND HABITAT Spawning occurs in late autumn and early winter, often during October and November, when water temperatures drop to between 44 and 48 degrees Fahrenheit. Browns prefer the headwaters of small, gravel-strewn streams, although lake-run fish have spawned on rocky shoals near the shoreline. In typical trout fashion, the female digs a nest with her tail into which eggs are deposited along with the male's sperm. Females five years of age average 2,000 eggs, which they cover with gravel. The young hatch the following spring. Lake and sea-run smolts usually remain in native rivers for at least one or two years before migrating to their "big water" environments. Brown trout are renowned for their carnivorous feeding habits. Native browns will forage above and below the water surface for

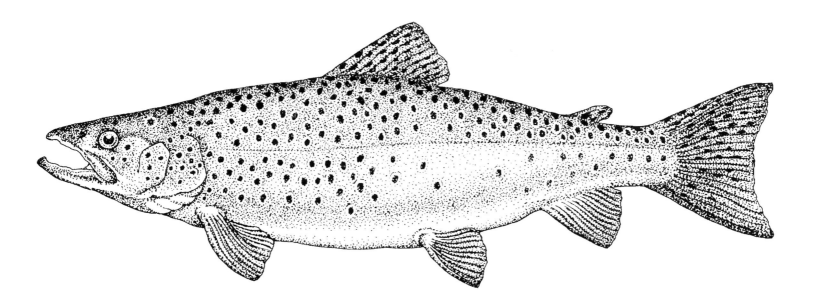

mayflies, caddis flies, stoneflies, and many others. They are also nocturnal feeders and will eat molluscs, frogs, crayfish, and various fish, including other trout. They have even been known to eat birds, mice, and other small mammals that wander into the water. The largest browns are often caught after dark. Anglers rate the brown as the wiliest of the stream trout for its caution and cleverness in concealment. Many believe that this high intelligence is the result of its European origins where centuries of intensive angling quickly culled away the inferior fish. The remaining genetic stock eventually produced browns that were superior in survival traits.

FISHING TACKLE Many methods are used to catch brown trout in lakes and streams. Native browns are pursued in rivers and streams by spinning enthusiasts, usually with ultra-light or medium-action gear and light lines. Spinners such as the Mepps Aglia or the Panther Martin and spoons such as the E.G.B. are cast with great accuracy to heavy cover in streams. To lure large

browns, bait-fishermen use frogs, minnows, worms, and crayfish. In the Great Lakes, browns are taken by salmon-trollers using electronic fish finders and downriggers with lures such as the Terminator or the Salmon Doctor. Shore fishermen experience great success casting

QUICK TIPS

1 Many times, shallow-water browns in large lakes are very wary of the troller's lures. It is necessary to run extremely long leads of a hundred yards or more. A better solution is to use a planer board, which presents the lure off to one side of the trolling boat. The boat then no longer scares the fish away from the lure.

2 If you've spotted a really big stream brown in some large pool and can't get it to hit your lure or bait, special tactics are called for. If it's a lunker you can hook a 2- to 3-inch creek chub lightly through the skin behind the dorsal fin, just to one side of the backbone. Another bait worth trying is a small frog hooked through one leg. The secret to success is timing. The best time to fish baits like this is at night. Be patient and wait for the fish to come to the bait. This technique is especially effective in big, slow pools found under railroad bridges or in large pools with deeply undercut banks.

3 Often an entire school of lake browns will come shoreward and roll about within casting distance without hitting artificials. Anglers even snag these fish accidentally. This is the time to rig a spawn bag under a slender float or through a sliding sinker on bottom. Again, patience is called for because this technique really works.

4 When fly-fishing for wily, native browns, anglers traditionally try to "match the hatch." The best way to find out what insects are plentiful around the stream is to tack a piece of flypaper to a nearby tree. After a few hours, check the paper and you'll have a pretty good idea of what the browns might be feeding on.

5 If you catch and keep a lake brown loaded with eggs and the fish are hitting on roe bags, don't miss your chance to stand out from the rest of the pack. Take some of the eggs and tie them into some sacking material. Browns seem to prefer fresh roe over cured or frozen eggs.

heavy spoons such as the Alligator or the Little Cleo. Often long, fairly flexible casting rods are used together with special, tapered-spool casting reels such as the Diawa Whisker or the Cardinal Ultracast. Fly-fishermen use both wet and dry flies, nymphs, and streamers.

FISHING TECHNIQUES. The fly-angler often views brown trout as being the ultimate quarry. Taking these exceedingly wary, native fish on a dry fly is very difficult. Since the brown tends to feed in quiet pools and runs, the fly-fisher must exercise great caution during the approach and presentation. When a rise is noticed on the water's surface, most anglers will routinely cast to it. Often this alone can frighten the fish away. If the fish shows any interest or continues feeding, however, the angler may switch patterns or drop to smaller flies. Great caution is required to ensure that the cast fly touches the water very, very gently. Favorite brown-trout flies are many and include famous names such as the Quill Gordon, March Brown, Blue Dun Spider, Hendrickson,

Native browns are known for their extreme caution. The experienced small-stream fisherman will spend most of the time fishing in areas that offer heavy cover for this shy trout. Concentrate on log jams, deep holes, and undercut banks. If you use lures, they must be retrieved very close to the cover. The angler must be prepared to take chances and lose lures to *snags. It is also a good idea to fish known brown hangouts after a fairly heavy rain, using a large lure such as a No. 4 Mepps Aglia. The murky water will likely embolden the otherwise wary fish into striking. Natural baits must be cast upstream from the cover and allowed to drift right under or alongside obstructions whenever possible. Lastly, make the* *odds work for you. Concentrate your fishing during the most probable times: early in the morning, late in the evening, or even at night.*

Royal Coachman, and Adams.

Spin-fishermen, too, can enjoy great sport with brown trout. In small streams, the angler often stalks his quarry for an entire season once he has observed a fish in a pool. Once hooked, stream browns mount spectacular battles and possess the uncanny ability to find line-breaking snags such as submerged branches or logs. Shore fishermen in lakes do not need to worry about stealth or careful presentation. They need only be present as the migratory browns arrive near the mouths of spawning rivers. Usually large schools will announce their presence by rolling or even jumping out of the water. They are very determined when striking lures, which are usually retrieved at fairly high speeds. Later in the season, migratory browns suddenly cease feeding, and lure-fishing begins to taper off. This is the bait-fisherman's time. Roe, worms, and sometimes minnows are fished beneath slender floats or on the bottom with sliding sinkers. When the fish are in the rivers, float-fishermen concentrate on the deeper and slower pools. River browns are frequently very loath to take baits. Anglers often resort to specialized 12- to 14-foot long rods that are specially designed for float-fishing with very light lines and 2- or even 1-pound-test leaders. This river-fishing style requires new baits. Various tiny insects and wet flies can be presented to spooky fish, and these novel methods often produce when all other methods fail.

Channel Catfish

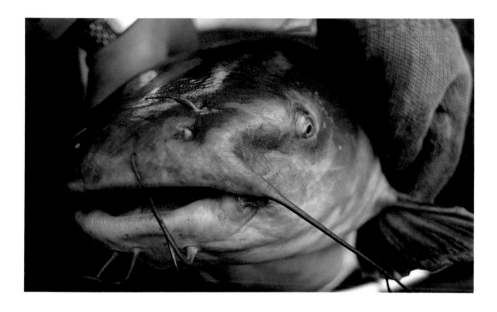

THEY MAY BE
UGLY, BUT THEY
TASTE GREAT
SMOKED!

COMMON NAMES channel catfish, Great Lake catfish, Great Lakes catfish, lake catfish, northern catfish, spotted catfish

DESCRIPTION The channel catfish has a much more carnivorous look about it than the other species of this family. Its sizable body is sleek, and there is very little of the "pot-bellied" look so characteristic of other catfishes, such as the brown bullhead. Like all catfishes, the channel cat possesses long barbels around its mouth: there are four under and two above the jaw. The lower jaw is dwarfed by a broad, flat head. Coloration may vary from blue or darkish silver to dark gray along the back of the fish. The channel cat's belly is usually whitish, and a number of irregular black spots are scattered along its often silvery sides. The tail is deeply forked, and the caudal fin possesses twenty-four to thirty rays, which, together with the spots on its sides, distinguishes the channel cat from close look-alikes such as the blue catfish and the white catfish.

SIZE The channel cat is the largest of the Canadian catfishes. Most mature fish weigh at least 3 or 4 pounds and reach lengths of 14 to 21 inches. These catfish can live up to twenty-four years in Canada and perhaps fourteen or so years in the faster-growing southern populations. In Canada, a very large channel cat weighs between 30 and 40 pounds, and these monster specimens are often caught in large waters, such as the Great Lakes, the St. Lawrence River, or the famous Red River system in Manitoba. The world-record

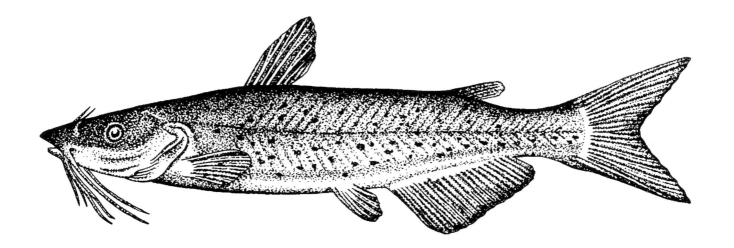

channel cat was taken in the United States, however, from the well-known Santee-Cooper Reservoir in South Carolina. It was caught in 1964 and weighed a scarcely believable 58 pounds!

DISTRIBUTION The channel catfish rarely wanders into salty waters. In the United States, its range extends over most of the central and eastern portions of the country, from the Great Lakes and the Saskatchewan River, southward to the northern shores of the Gulf of Mexico. In Canada, the channel cat is at home in the St. Lawrence system, the Ottawa River, the Great Lakes, and portions of southern Ontario, including Lake Nipissing and the French River. It is also present in southern Manitoba, notably in the waters of Lake Winnipeg and Lake Manitoba.

BEHAVIOR AND HABITAT Channel catfish usually spawn later in the spring when water temperatures climb to 75 degrees Fahrenheit or higher. Although they will spawn in still waters, many cats will migrate into

rivers. Channel catfish lay great numbers of eggs, some 4,000 for a female of 1 to 4 pounds in weight. The eggs are laid in a hidden area, such as an undercut bank, log pile, or among rocks, and the males will guard this site diligently until the eggs hatch. The young grow more

QUICK TIPS

1 *Channel cats take baits very firmly, so there's not much need to let them "run" with the bait. The rod should point at ten o'clock until a cat hits the bait. Next, lower the tip to the water in order to give a bit of line and then set the hook hard.*

2 *Don't overlook structures such as dams in the spring for spawning channel cats. It is common to catch ten or fifteen fish a day when they're running heavily. During the day the fish hold right at the base of the dams. As light levels decrease, look for them in the fast-flowing shallow water.*

3 *When the cats aren't biting, try making your presentation more natural by drifting your bait past them. Put your line through a slip float so that the line can slide through. As the float drifts downriver, free spool line as necessary so the bait is just off the bottom, touching the odd rock or boulder. When a fish hits, close the bail and set the hook.*

4 *In winding rivers, always look for big channel cats in the deepest pools, which are usually found in the bends of the river. Often this spot has the added attraction of an undercut bank.*

5 *To get a very effective stink bait, just lay some chicken livers out in the sun for a few days. You won't like the aroma but the channel cats will just love it!*

rapidly in southern portions of their range, and many reach sexual maturity at between five and eight years of age.

Channel catfish are most at home in lakes and fairly large rivers. They seek out the clear and cool deeper water that is not usually inhabited by their smaller relative, the brown bullhead. They are found over a sand or gravel bottom and seldom occur in turbid, mud-bottom areas such as shallow bays.

They avoid strong light by lurking beneath cover during the day. They are most active at sunrise, sunset and at night, and this is usually when anglers will try for them. Channel cats are omnivorous and feed on a generous variety of plants and animals. Although these catfish are most often bottom feeders, they will pursue prey near the surface of the water as well. Like other catfishes they use their excellent sense of taste to run down their prey, yet

In many areas, savvy anglers use homemade concoctions called "stink baits," which can be very effective. They are also invariably very, very smelly and consist of fish, meat, and various other savory ingredients that have been allowed to rot. An appropriately-sized sponge is placed on the hook and then dipped into the goop (you don't have to actually touch it) before being used to attract big channel cats. As unpleasant as it may seem, cat-fishermen swear by it.

evidence suggests that they also depend heavily on sight. Mayflies, caddis flies, crayfish, green algae, various water plants, and a wide variety of fishes, such as minnows and yellow perch, are all food sources for the channel cat.

FISHING TACKLE Heavier rod-and-reel combinations are recommended for this very large catfish. A fiberglass or graphite spinning rod in the 7- to 9-foot range or a medium to heavy bait-casting outfit will do nicely. The reel should be able to carry some 200 to 300 yards of line. The line itself should be at least 15-pound test, and a 20-pound-test safety margin is advisable since these fish often inhabit fast water that magnifies their already considerable strength. Bait-fishing requires sturdy hooks and a variety of sinkers for bottom-fishing. Channel cats will also eagerly strike lures, especially in the faster waters found below dams or rapids. They have been known to take spoons such as a red and white Daredevle or a silver Alligator, spinners such as a Mepps Aglia or a silver Olympique, as well as plugs such as a Rapala Floating Original or an A C Shiner.

FISHING TECHNIQUES Once the angler has located a channel cat hot-spot, he can confidently look forward to some exciting fishing. The very best time is at night and, in general, bait-fishing outperforms lure-fishing. Hook sizes should be chosen to match the size of the bait and should be more or less buried in the bait with only the barb and point showing. The best setup consists of a sliding sinker rig – the line is passed through an egg or bell sinker until about 12 to 16 inches protrude. A small split-shot sinker is then pinched on the line near the sliding sinker, and a hook is tied on the end of the line. This will allow a catfish to pick up the bait and move off without feeling the weight of the heavy sinker. Frequently the area to be fished is "chummed" carefully with fragrant foods that are dumped into the water, often by the bucketfull. This attracts the fish from long distances and

concentrates them in the target zone. Anglers often collect bait fish that are abundant in their area, such as smelt, which run in huge schools and can easily be collected in bulk. These fish are chopped up, together with chicken entrails and some type of bulking material such as bread. Many fishermen add a bottle of cod-liver oil to further improve the scent trail. This delightful mixture (for a channel cat) is then either dumped overboard or placed into fine mesh netting so the smell can "leach" away without actually feeding the catfish. The actual baits used vary from angler to angler, and "can't miss" recipes are jealously guarded secrets. Many anglers simply use dead frogs, smelt, shad, freshwater herring, suckers, worms, or just about any dead or live bait that is available. And, indeed, channel catfish are not finicky feeders and will often smash the bait rather than cautiously "mouthing" it. Channel cats are very underrated as fighters. They are more than capable of testing angler and tackle to the limit, especially when they are very large and/or when they are caught in fast-flowing waters.

THE TOOLS OF THE TRADE.

Chinook Salmon

A GREAT LAKES
TROPHY TAKEN
JUST AFTER
DUSK.

COMMON NAMES blackmouth, chinook, chinook salmon, king salmon, smilie, spring, spring salmon, tyee

DESCRIPTION No other west-coast or Great Lakes salmon is sought with the same fervor as the chinook. Adult chinook sport iridescent green to green-blue backs, silvery sides, and silver-to-white bellies. They are also dotted with spots on their body and on all fins. Their mouths are typically black, hence the name "blackmouth." Their black mouths, heavily spotted tails, and their distinctive thyme odor distinguish them from coho salmon. Chinook darken when spawning in rivers, becoming almost black in many cases, and the males develop prominent "kypes" or jaws that are used in fights with other males over the right to spawn with females.

SIZE Chinook are caught year-round, and size often depends on time of year. Many winter chinook of the west coast weigh in at 8 to 10 pounds in March. By May, a 20-pounder may be considered a good catch. Summer and fall seem to provide the largest chinook for west-coast and Great Lakes anglers, when catches of tyee or salmon weighing more than 30 pounds become more common.

The long-standing record for British Columbia is a 92-pound, 58.5-inch chinook caught in the Skeena River in 1959. A world-record

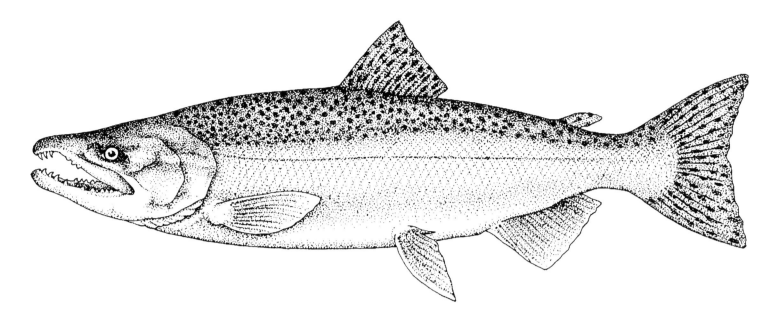

hatchery-reared chinook of 80.5 pounds was caught in 1990 in River's Inlet by Washington angler David McIlveen. Two fish weighing more than 120 pounds have been caught by commercial fishermen in Alaska. Even though there have been many stories of the 50-pounders that got away, the chinook fishing in the Great Lakes has been simply fantastic. Back in 1980, Raymo Polidoro landed a 45.38-pound trophy.

DISTRIBUTION The chinook salmon is a native of the Pacific Ocean, from the Ventura River in southern California, north to Point Hope, Alaska. Chinook spawn in more than 250 streams and rivers in British Columbia. They spawn more than 560 miles upstream in the Fraser drainage, and more than 1,200 miles up the Yukon River. Chinook also occur in northeast Asia, from northern Hokkaido, Japan, to the Anadyr River, USSR.

Chinook have been introduced in many parts of the United States as well as in Mexico, Argentina, Chile, Nicaragua, England, Ireland, Holland, France, Germany, Italy, Hawaii, Australia, Tasmania, and New Zealand. The most famous and successful introductions of chinook occurred in the Great Lakes, where there is a booming sport fishery.

SCOTT RIPLEY

BEHAVIOR AND HABITAT Chinook in the Pacific are "feeding machines," capable of putting on 50 to 60 or more pounds within two or three years. They feed ravenously on herring, anchovies, needlefish, shrimp, and other plankton and fish. Underwater video cameras have recorded chinook engaged in feeding frenzies around "balls" of herring. The chinook typically hunt out herring in the lees of islands, around underwater ledges, and other areas that concentrate bait fish, then herd them toward the surface in "balls." They will then slash through the school and around its edges, and pick off wounded and dead fish as they sink to the bottom.

Habitats and food of chinook in the Great Lakes differ from those of Pacific fish. In spring and early summer, before the lake is thermally stratified, most chinook are found within 2.5 miles of the shore at intermediate depths of 16 or more feet of water. In the heat of summer, however, most chinook move into deeper water. While in these habitats, chinook feed almost exclusively on rainbow smelt.

On the west coast, fattened adult chinook move inshore near spawning rivers over most of the year. Salmon occur year-round near such major spawning tributaries as the Fraser River, but maximum numbers of spawners do not build up until August and September.

Great Lakes salmon start to

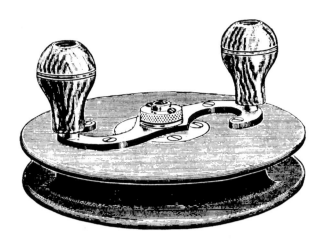

concentrate near river mouths by August. Salmon by the thousands will "stage" for several weeks preparing themselves for their annual runs. Actual spawning occurs between September and October. This, of course, is one of the most popular times to angle for Great Lake giants since shallow water makes them accessible.

Chinook tend to spawn in deeper water and on larger gravel than other Pacific salmon. The redd or nest may be more than 9 feet long. Eggs laid in the fall hatch the following spring. Most of the fry then spend a year in fresh water before migrating to sea.

FISHING TACKLE More chinook are probably taken by trolling than by any other method. Downriggers and flashers are standard gear for west-coast and Great Lakes anglers. Flashers include the ever-popular Hot Spot and the O'ki. Many anglers also prefer dodgers, such as the well-known Jensen Dodger.

Chinook anglers normally use a wide variety of terminal tackle. Popular west-coast baits are an-chovies and herring, including "cut plugs" and "strips." Spoons are very popular in the Great Lakes, and to a lesser degree on the west coast. Plugs are also favorites of trollers, including such famous brands as J-Plugs and Tomics. Other productive artificials include the Apex Hot Spot and the Ross Swimmer Tail. Thousands of chinook are also caught on trolled hoochies, which are squid or octopus imitations. Green and white are productive colors and, in B.C., so is pink. Last but not least, many chinook anglers jig for their quarry, using Buzz Bombs, ZZingers, and other imitators of wounded bait fish.

Many west-coast anglers also "mooch" live and dead bait fish for chinook. A banana weight keeps the bait down, and a rod with a limber and sensitive tip is used to detect the often subtle takes of these giants.

In fresh water, most west-coast and Great Lakes salmon fishers catch chinook with roe or roe imitations. Roe is drifted under floats or bottom-bounced to the salmon. Chinook also hit a variety of spinners and spoons in various colors.

SCOTT RIPLEY

1 When the chinook aren't hitting your offerings at the other end of the downrigger, try lengthening your lead. This is especially important if the salmon are, in fact, showing up on the sonar. A normal distance between cannonball and lure is about 15 or 20 feet. Try extending that distance to 40 to 60 feet to pick up fish that are too spooky to hit normal presentations.

2 One of the problems encountered in downrigger fishing for chinook occurs because the current speeds near the water's surface can be quite different from those at lower depths. This means that a lure that runs perfectly on the surface may wobble too quickly if a fast subsurface current is running opposite to the boat's movement. The lure may also move too slowly if a fast subsurface current is running with the boat. The solution is simple. Always use lures that provide a lively action over a wide range of speeds (such as the J-Plug) so that the effects of unpredictable subsurface currents are minimized.

3 Chinook, especially immature salmon called jacks, are fond of eating each other's eggs. In the river, pairs of chinook can often be spotted on a redd or nest. If there's a pool or run below such a spawning pair, get your rod ready with a small spawn bag or even a single egg as bait. If there's an "egg eater" greedily at work, it will be particularly vulnerable to this presentation.

4 Don't neglect the use of lures when chinook barge into the rivers. It's suspected that chinook, particularly the males, will angrily charge flashy spoons, spinners, and even large plugs that annoy them, such as the J13 Rapala.

5 There are a few ways to increase your odds when fishing for chinook near harbors. Use spoons because they cast farther without as much effort as plugs or spinners. Always spread your casts out in a fan shape to cover more water. Finally, hold your rod tip pointing at the direction of the cast and just above the water's surface so you'll be able to get a good hook set.

FISHING TECHNIQUES Trolling is the top producer for chinook. Trolling covers lots of water, you can troll where the fish are thanks to electronic fish finders, and several rods can be trolled at one time, each running a different lure to find what works best. Trollers often stick around the mouths of major spawning rivers and wherever baitfish are concentrated.

Again, angling preferences are often divided between dodgers, with their side-to-side action, and the rotating flashers. Spoons are fished flasher free, and many anglers prefer not to battle flasher and salmon. Straight bait or artificials often produce well when salmon are aggressively feeding, though the added enticement of dodgers and flashers seems to be called for when salmon are close to spawning.

Nonfeeding salmon in rivers also seem to need waking up, with large chunks of roe, brightly colored flies, or vibrating and flashing spoons or spinners. Even with these enticements, repeated casting is the norm to attract salmon and maintain steady action.

A GORGEOUS CHINOOK FROM THE KENAI RIVER IN ALASKA.

Chum Salmon

COMMON NAMES autumn salmon, chum, chum salmon, dog, dog salmon

DESCRIPTION The chum or dog salmon is not a primary target of most salmon anglers in Canada, largely because chum are not considered to be a sport fish there. Nevertheless, thousands are caught each year by west-coast sport fishermen, targeting coho and chinook salmon, and these "incidental" fish often provide more action and grander battles than the so-called sport fish.

Chum are typically large and hard to control, even with heavy gear. Twenty-pound tackle busters are commonly caught on many west-coast rivers and streams. Males are easily recognized by their large kypes and the olive green and purple bars and blotches that adorn their sides. The caudal, anal, and pectoral fins are tipped with black and white. All in all, spawning chum are one of the most colorful salmon to test the tackle of river anglers.

SIZE Most chum salmon in British Columbia mature at age three or four. By this time, the majority weigh more than 10 pounds. The average size of fish returning to spawn in one B.C. study was just under 12 pounds, with some individual fish weighing up to 45 pounds. Males typically grow faster and larger than females.

DISTRIBUTION Maturing chum roam the Pacific and Arctic oceans, the Sea of Japan, and the Okhotsk and Bering seas from the Sacramento River in California to Pusan, Korea. In the Arctic Ocean, chum are found west to the Lena River, and

SEPTEMBER IS THE BEST TIME TO RIVER FISH FOR CHUM.

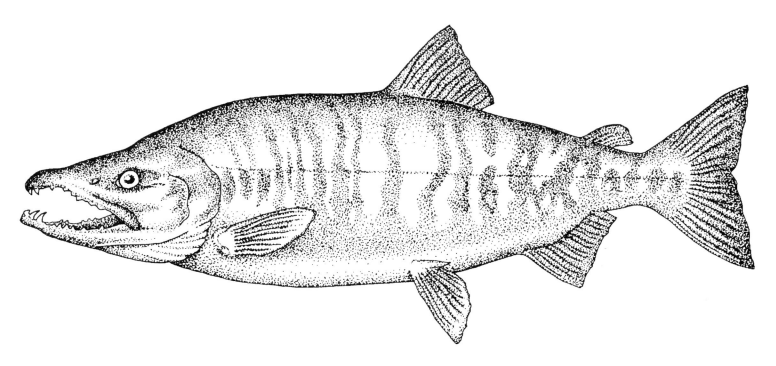

east to at least the Peel and Mackenzie rivers. Chum migrate up the Mackenzie to the rapids below Fort Smith on the Slave River, and also enter Great Bear Lake. Millions also migrate up the Fraser River and hundreds of other rivers in British Columbia.

The chum holds the distinction of being the least frequently introduced of the Pacific salmon. Eggs from Puget Sound were planted in 1955 into the Winisk River, which drains into Hudson Bay. In that same year, fingerlings from a hatchery in Thunder Bay were released into the Attawapiskat River, which flows into James Bay. Both introductions failed.

BEHAVIOR AND HABITAT Chum fry feed on a variety of insects, crustaceans, and worm-like organisms in fresh water, but, in general, they spend so little time in fresh water that most food studies have focused on marine ecosystems. At sea, chum salmon eat a wide variety of marine organisms, including crustaceans, various fishes, and squid.

Chum mature and return to rivers to spawn, usually in their third or fourth year of life. Like most salmon, they seldom feed in fresh water compared to other resident species of river fishes. Chum readily take salmonid eggs, making real or artificial roe imitations and colored wool good bets for anglers.

THE HANDSOME
OLIVE GREEN
AND PURPLE
BARS MAKE
CHUM EASILY
RECOGNIZABLE.

In northern British Columbia, chum arrive on spawning grounds as early as July. Farther south they start to arrive at stream mouths in September, and they may not reach spawning grounds until December. They are usually thick in the Fraser River and many of its tributaries in October and November. Chum are notorious for arriving in spawning grounds in advanced states of sexual maturity – highly colored, and often showing the signs of decomposition commonly associated with late-spawning salmon. These characteristics no doubt decrease their appeal to sport anglers, and also mean that many chum spawn soon after reaching rivers, often in tidal areas. Chum are less able to navigate past obstacles than are the other Pacific salmon, and consequently, most "dogs" rarely migrate farther upstream than 90 miles. The Yukon River is one notable exception, and the main run moves upstream to spawn above Dawson in late September, a distance of some 1,200 miles.

Male chum are typically aggressive on the spawning grounds. Chum build redds that average more than 2 square yards, usually in medium-size gravel. Females generally lay between 2,400 and 3,100 eggs, with eggs hatching from late December through late February. The fry emerge from the gravel in April and May, with most migrating to sea immediately, where they form schools in saltwater estuaries.

FISHING TACKLE Since chum are not small, tackle should be fairly stout.

Q U I C K   T I P S

1 When the chum arrive at river mouths (usually in November and December), they will take artificial lures such as wobbling plugs. The secret is to use color patterns that contain red or fluorescent orange.

2 Often chum are found in small pockets or runs that cannot be drift-fished because of their size and the many nearby rocks. Don't pass up these tiny holding pools. In such close confines, simply step near the pocket, pull out a short length of line, and drop the bait vertically into the hole in a "dunking" fashion.

3 Chum salmon are egg eaters, so what better bait than natural spawn? Even chunks of spawn with the skein still attached are a highly effective bait. Anglers often pass the line through the eye of the hook and snell it on to the hook bend. This creates a kind of loop between the eye and the bend, which can be tightened around the hooked roe chunk to keep it from falling off the hook.

4 In a pinch, cheese rolled into a tiny ball or even kernels of corn will serve as a salmon-egg imitation for pinks.

5 To increase the attraction of your egg baits, add a piece of brightly colored Styrofoam, such as the Lil' Corky, above the hook. These tiny balls resemble single eggs and will also increase the buoyancy of your roe bag, keeping it from snagging on the bottom.

Most west-coast anglers use 10 1/2-foot drifting rods, or fly rods that are appropriate for steelhead and chinook. A 15-pound test mainline and 10-pound test leaders will be tested to the limit by 20-pound chum, especially where currents are fast. Similarly, chum can straighten even the finest 1/0 hooks, so don't use anything smaller unless you don't mind replacing numerous hooks.

FISHING TECHNIQUES Chum readily take roe, Gooey Bobs, Jensen Eggs, colored beads, or other roe imitations. Fluorescent yarn is another hot bet in pink, chartreuse, orange, salmon, red, or most other colors. Various spoons, spinners, and many patterns of flies may also produce hits.

Paradoxically, most river anglers in B.C. try to avoid catching chum while they are fishing for coho and chinook. Chum are notorious bait thieves and time robbers – time to land and release them, and time needed to replace snapped leaders and bent hooks. However, many of these anglers, whether they admit it or not, often welcome the challenging diversion of chum. They are frequently caught among coho and chinook so the angler does not need to go out of his way to catch them. They hit especially well in rapids, a favorite fishing site for savvy anglers targeting coho. They also hit well in pools, riffles, slack water and generally in more places than coho and chinook. Their aggressive nature and large size combine to make them a deliberate target for an up-and-coming group of anglers armed with fly rods.

SCIENTIFIC NAME *Oncorhynchus kisutch*

Coho Salmon

COMMON NAMES blueback, coho, coho salmon, silvers, silver salmon

DESCRIPTION The coho is one of the most sought-after salmonids in North America. Maturing coho have steel-blue to slightly green backs, and their sides are brilliant silver, hence the name "silver salmon." Coho can be confused with chinook salmon, though coho generally have whiter gums and fewer spots on their tails than chinook. Chinook also sport an unmistakable odor similar to that of thyme. Breeding male coho have a dark blue-green back and head, a gray-black belly, and red-striped sides. During the late stages of spawning, males can be almost entirely red, and their kypes and humped backs are well formed. The males use the kypes when fighting other males for females, and the humps help to protect them from other males' attacks.

SIZE The vast majority of mature adult coho taken by sport fishermen probably weigh between 5 and 10 pounds. Coho grow much larger, however, with many sport-caught fish regularly weighing in in the mid to high teens. The forty-year-old world record for coho, a 31-pound fish from Cowichan Bay in British Columbia, was surpassed in 1989 by a coho from New York. On September 27, Jerry Lifton landed a 33.4-pound all-tackle-record coho from the Salmon River. This fish, however, will be hard to beat.

DISTRIBUTION The coho occurs naturally only in the Pacific Ocean and its tributary rivers and streams, from Monterey Bay, California, to Port Hope, Alaska. The coho has also been introduced to many freshwater-lake systems throughout North America. The most famous freshwater introductions are those of the Great Lakes. Between 1873 and 1878, thousands of coho fry were released in Lake Erie and its tributaries in Ontario, Ohio, and Michigan. The program failed, however. The first successful program started in Michigan in 1966, followed by Ohio and New York (1968), and Ontario (1969). These stocks are presently maintained

JIM MARKOU

A BROWN BEAR SHARES ITS EXPERTISE WITH A SURPRISED FISHERMAN.

mostly by fish culture, and coho now occur in large numbers in all of the Great Lakes.

BEHAVIOR AND HABITAT Young coho in Alaska's fresh waters enjoy a varied diet of fly larvae, stoneflies, beetles, caddis flies, worms, and spiders. When smolts enter the sea, they feed on other salmon fry, herring, various other fishes, squid, shrimp, and other plankton. Adults in the Pacific eat herring, anchovy, capelin, coho, lanternfish, hake, rockfishes, squid, shrimp, crab larvae, and other plankton. Adult coho in the Great Lakes feed primarily on rainbow smelt and alewife.

Coho typically spawn in small, gravelly streams. Adults usually school at the mouths of rivers, moving upstream when fall rains raise water levels. Spawning runs in the Great Lakes occur mainly in September and October. West-coast coho spawn at similar times, though fresh-run coho in some streams continue migrating well into December. Spawning takes place in swift water.

Adult coho in the Pacific and in the Great Lakes are often taken by anglers near the mouths of spawning rivers. Pacific-coast anglers also search for coho around tide lines, in kelp beds, and in the lee (tidal or current) of small islands and underwater ledges. Coho in the Great Lakes are often found in all depths of water.

FISHING TACKLE Coho salmon are taken on a wide variety of tackle. Fresh or cured salmon roe is the top choice of many river anglers. Brightly colored wool is also a good bet in rivers, especially where currents are swift. Pink, red, orange, and chartreuse are good colors. Spoons and spinners in red, silver, and copper are favorite lures.

Spoons are another good bet in both the Pacific and the Great Lakes. A pink and white Ross Swimmer Tail, developed for commercial coho fishing, has also proved effective for sport anglers. Anchovies and herring strips are other top bait choices of many west-coast anglers. Coho are also jigged with such standbys as the Buzz

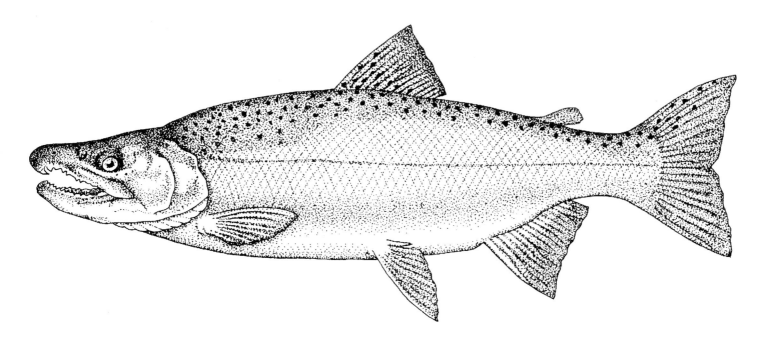

Bomb and ZZinger. Finally, coho provide excellent sport on quickly trolled "bucktail" flies, with green and white and other color combinations proving effective. This technique is so popular that bucktail tournaments are popping up along the west coast of North America.

FISHING TECHNIQUES Techniques for catching coho in rivers vary according to region and individual preferences. Most river anglers in British Columbia use roe or roe imitations fished under a styrofoam float. Floats are easily guided, using long rods, to various lies. They also reduce the number of snags encountered in comparison to the "bottom-bouncing" techniques popular in Washington, Oregon, and the Great Lakes tributaries. Casting spoons and spinners are also highly popular among river anglers. Casts are made upstream, and the lures are allowed to drift across and down the current.

Trolling is the mainstay of coho anglers in the Great Lakes and in saltwater areas of the Pacific Coast. Fast trolling speeds (5 to 7 knots)

and lively topwater lure action are the most productive. Rods should be light enough to allow for a sporting battle, yet stiff enough to set the hook and to control fish that can easily top 10 pounds. Downriggers are standard for getting lures down to the coho, and

slide down the main line until it reaches the "belly" created by the trolling movement. Now you have two opportunities to catch a coho.

4 Coho salmon are great fighters and have the unusual habit of wrapping themselves around the line by spinning their bodies in the water. This often leads to lines being severed on sharp gill plates so it's often necessary to tie on a leader. Use an 18- to 36-inch length of 20- to 30-pound test line. This leader can then be attached to a barrel swivel tied to the main line and will prevent broken lines.

5 When you're fighting a coho in a large lake, remember that there's no need to hurry the fight or take any risks. As long as the fish is not threatening to spool off all of your line, there is really no possibility for it to create problems such as snagging up your line. All you have to do is allow the fish to run and gently "pump" it back toward you when it slows down. By taking your time and repeating this sequence you will seldom lose a fish.

1 One of the best ways to entice coho using multiple downriggers is to run an entire set of spoons to imitate a school of bait fish. To really fool the fish, bend one of the lures so that its action is impaired slightly. This makes it resemble an injured bait fish, which often becomes the target of marauding cohos.

2 In shallow water the troller can run flat lines near the surface, often far behind the boat, to minimize scaring the

fish. The most effective method is to troll in S-patterns, which cause the lure to alternately speed up and slow down.

3 The downrigger angler can make each of his rods more effective by rigging "stackers." Simply tie snap swivels to both ends of a 4-foot length of 20- to 30-pound test line. Place a spoon into one snap swivel and loop the other around the main line before snapping it back on its own stacker line. This stacker will

S P E C I A L   T I P

Once coho have spent some time in the river and have become highly colored in preparation to spawn, they can be quite difficult to catch because they are less interested in food. For difficult fish, a marabou or bucktail jig is the answer.

Look for the coho in deep pools and fish the jig very slowly across the bottom, almost dragging it at times. Productive colors include purple, red, white, and black, and favorite sizes range from 1/8 to 3/4 ounces.

fish finders are useful for determining the correct depth. Trollers on the west coast have also had great success with bucktail flies trolled on the surface.

Two other popular angling techniques are mooching with live bait and jigging. Moochers use small fish, light banana weights of 4 or more ounces, and long, limber rods that help anglers detect light takes. Jigging is one of the most enjoyable ways of catching coho, since the battle is not encumbered by weights or flashers. Standard river rods are used to flutter to resemble wounded bait fish.

Finally, coho are excellent targets for fly-fishers. These fish hit a wide variety of flies, including egg imitations, and a vast array of small flies in red, green, orange, and black. A 5-weight rod with a sink-tip line is a good choice for smaller fish; larger rods may be needed when fishing for large fish.

SCIENTIFIC NAMES Black crappie: *Pomoxis nigromaculatus*
White crappie: *Pomoxis annularis*

Crappie

COMMON NAMES Black crappie: bachelor perch, calico bass, grass bass, moonfish, Oswego bass, papermouth, shiner, speckled bass, strawberry bass

White crappie: bachelor perch, crawpie, papermouth, silver bass, white bass

DESCRIPTION These fish with their odd names belong to the *Centrarchidore* or sunfish family. Despite their names, both the white and the black crappie are very similar in shape and color, and it takes a discerning eye indeed to tell them apart. The black crappie has a noticeably *irregular* pattern of spots on its body, whereas the white crappie has seven to nine pale vertical bars on its side. Black crappie also have seven or eight spines on their front dorsal fin, while white crappie always have six. Although both species are also very similar in appearance to other sunfish, they have larger mouths and a pointed gill cover. The mouth parts are, however, quite delicate; for this reason, the crappie are often called "papermouths."

SIZE Most black crappie taken by anglers are less than 12 inches long and weigh less then 2 pounds, although a lunker of 4 pounds, 8 ounces was caught in Kerr Lake, Virginia.

White crappie average 6 to 12 inches in length and generally weigh between 1/4 and 1 pound. Several fish of over 5 pounds have been recorded, however, and the world record stands at an impressive 5 pounds, 3 ounces, from the Enid Dam on the Mississippi River.

DISTRIBUTION Both species frequently inhabit the same waters and have been widely transplanted throughout North America. The black crappie's range is in the eastern United States from the Quebec border to and including Alabama, Texas, and Florida. In Canada, it is found in southern Quebec, Ontario, Manitoba, and British Columbia.

The white crappie is common in the entire eastern half of the United States, from the Quebec border to northern Mexico, although it is noticeably scarce throughout most of Florida. In Canada, the white crappie is much less abundant than the

A HAPPY ANGLER WITH AN HOUR'S CATCH OF CRAPPIE.

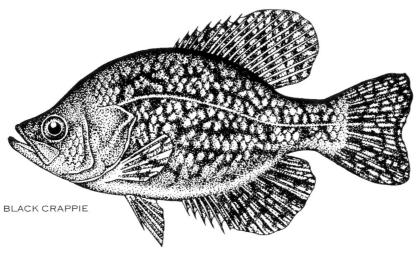

BLACK CRAPPIE

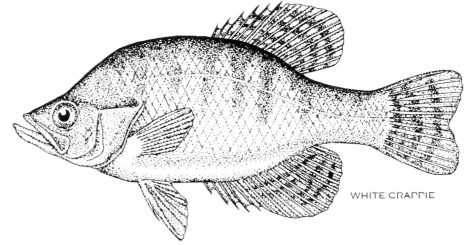

WHITE CRAPPIE

black crappie and is limited to areas in Ontario near western Lake Ontario, Lake Erie, Lake St. Clair, and parts of Lake Huron.

BEHAVIOR AND HABITAT The black crappie prefers large ponds and shallow lakes, or rivers with sand or mud bottoms. It frequents quiet, clear waters, often with ample vegetation.

The white crappie favors more silted and turbid waters and will thrive over soft or hard bottoms. It is most at home in reservoirs, bayous, and rivers of the southern United States. There are a few variances in the behavior of the two species. Black crappie are fond of traveling in schools and will spawn in shallow waters. Spawning occurs in water temperatures of 62 to 65 degrees Fahrenheit and may occur as early as January in the south or as late as June in the north. Because the males will guard the spawning nests, the crappie has earned the charming name of "bachelor perch." Most spawning is conducted on gravel in water depths of 2 to 10 feet. They will also spawn near weed beds, beneath undercut banks,

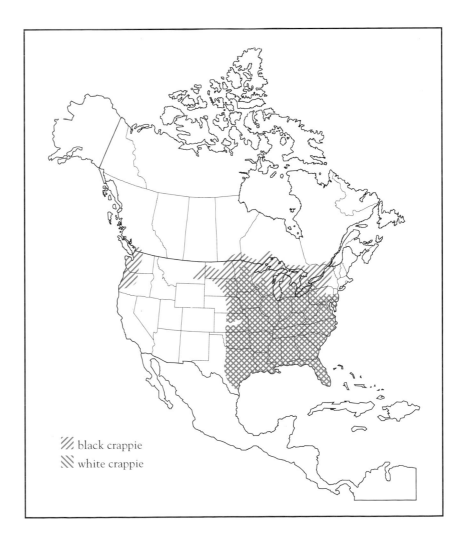

///// black crappie
\\\\\ white crappie

or alongside boulders and logs.

Crappies are much more sensitive to light than other sunfish and will thus feed most actively during dusk or dawn, or even at night. Feeding slows down at water temperatures below 50 degrees Fahrenheit. Both crappie species are equipped with gill rakers, which they use to strain planktonic organisms from the water. Larger crappie will also prey on aquatic insects, crustaceans, and other fishes such as gizzard or threadfin shad.

FISHING TACKLE Closed-face or open-face reels and sensitive rods in the 4- to 5-foot range are often used by the most dedicated crappie fishermen. Many of these ultra-light rods weigh less than 4 ounces and are made with graphite or boron for extra sensitivity. Great care should be taken to match rods and reels to create a balanced combination. These light outfits are ideal for casting the tiny lures and baits used for crappies. Once again a large variety of lures are effective. Small spinners, spoons, and plugs will work, but the favorite lures by far are the various kinds of jigs and jig-spinner combinations. Jigs such as Gaspen's Ugly Bug, Northland's Whistler, or simply a 1/16-ounce marabou are very popular. Jig-spinner combinations such as the Beetle Spin or the Whistler Spin are very effective as well. Crappies also seem to be made for bait-fishing, and here the lowly bobber comes in handy. Bobbers are even used in conjunction with jigs and bait.

FISHING TECHNIQUES Crappies are much more shy and cautious of disturbances than the other sunfish-family members. On some days they will bite readily; on other days they become strangely reluctant. It therefore becomes necessary for the angler to use light lines and to move about with a measure of stealth. Bait-fishing is often conducted with 4-pound test line and No. 4 or 6 hooks baited with 1- to 2-inch minnows hooked through the tail, back, or lips. This rig is suspended from a sensitive float near likely cover, such as weed beds, boulders, or brush piles. Other effective live baits include strips of fish meat,

QUICK TIPS

1 *If you live near good crappie lakes or ponds, check them every few days in the spring so that you don't miss the big early-season run. It only lasts a few weeks in most places, and you'll want to take advantage of the action as much as possible.*

2 *Use some fine wire hooks that are extremely sharp when fishing for crappies. Their paper-thin mouths can easily tear if you have to put too much pressure on them when setting the hook.*

3 *Some of the lightest jigs in the 1/8 to 1/64 ounce sizes are*

most productive for fishing crappies.

4 *If you are fishing known crappie-holding water but are not getting any action, be patient. Often the fish will move in all of a sudden and feed quickly, then move out again. You have to stay and*

wait them out in order to get in on the fast-paced bonanza.

5 *As with other game fish, try to release most of the very biggest crappies. This way, the larger fish that have superior genes may go on to spawn superior offspring for generations to come.*

---

garden worms, leeches, grasshoppers, crickets, and mayfly nymphs. Baits are especially effective when they are stealthily presented to spawning crappie near stumps, logs, weed beds, or brush areas.

Often these baits are used to tip the various lures used for crappies. Indeed, spinners such the Comet-Mino already have an imitation minnow over the hooks. Lures are especially effective when they are cast to fish-holding spots such as flooded timber and brush. Other likely spots include weed edges, island points, rock piles, and areas close to boathouses and bridge pilings. Once a school is found,

crappies can often be caught in large numbers. The angler should choose lures that are not easily snagged and that work well on a fairly slow retrieve. A crappie strike may be a fairly subtle affair, so the angler must stay alert.

Fly-rodding has, of course, become a very popular style of crappie fishing. Often 2-weight fly rods are used with 6x leaders with small nymphs and wet flies.

Crappies are even caught through the ice. Holes are usually located over dropoffs, flats, or points. Light-action rods are used with bottom-bait rigs, bait-float rigs, or jigging lures such as the Kastmaster.

Cutthroat Trout

ANOTHER
BEAUTIFUL CUTT
IS FOUGHT OUT!

SCOTT RIPLEY

COMMON NAMES Clark's trout, coastal cutthroat, coastal cutthroat trout, cutt, cutthroat trout, lake trout, red-throated trout, sea trout, short-tailed trout, Yellowstone cutthroat

DESCRIPTION The cutthroat is much coveted by anglers. It has a characteristically trout-like body, which is both streamlined and powerful. The tail is somewhat forked and the head slightly pointed. A slight kype or hook develops in the jaws of the males during the spawning season. The fish has acquired its peculiar name from a suggestive crimson slash that runs along the lower jaw. The numerous subspecies account for variations in color patterns among regional populations of cutthroat. Often the pectoral fins are red, while the pelvic and anal fins possess red leading edges. Most cutthroat have spots on their silvery sides, and these are sometimes sparse and dark and at other times numerous and faint. The back may vary in color from a green to a yellow-green. Coloration and identification are often complicated since the cutthroat hybridizes with both rainbow and golden trout. Because of variations between subspecies, most anglers rely on the distinctive crimson jaw slash to identify the cutthroat.

SIZE Since cutthroat are found in fresh waters and the sea, the average weights of sea-run versus freshwater specimens will vary. Freshwater cutthroat will usually weigh between 2 and 6 pounds, while the sea-run versions are often larger and weigh between 5 and 10 pounds although 4- to 5-pound fish are average. Numerous cutthroat in the 15- to 20-pound class have been recorded, especially in Nevada and California. In fact, the world-record cutthroat, taken in 1925, weighed a staggering 41 pounds, and came from Pyramid Lake, California; it belonged to the largest subspecies of this trout, the Lahontan cutthroat.

DISTRIBUTION The cutthroat's range is confined to the western coastal area of North America. Along the west coast proper, it is found from the Eel River in California all the way to Seward, Alaska, and has been

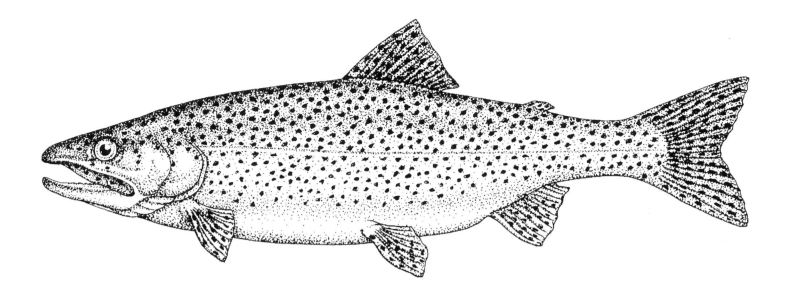

introduced in Colorado and New Mexico. In Canada, the cutthroat occurs along the entire western coastline of British Columbia. In the interior, cutthroat species are also found in southeastern British Columbia and in western Alberta.

BEHAVIOR AND HABITAT Anadromous or sea-run cutthroat will migrate up-river in their native rivers to spawn in late autumn or early winter. The mating pairs search out small streams with gravel bottoms, and the female lays between 1,100 and 1,700 eggs in a redd or nest that she has made by turning sideways and fluttering her tail. At this time, males will behave aggressively toward other males. After the eggs have been fertilized by the male, the female thrashes her tail upstream from the redd to cover the eggs with several inches of gravel. After six or seven weeks, the eggs hatch and the perilous life of the fry begins. They move into larger rivers or lakes and often reach the sea after two or three years. Once they reach the sea, cutthroat remain near the coastlines, usually in estuaries,

where they often mingle with salmon. They will remain in this brackish estuary water, which is a mix of salty seawater and fresh river water. Sexual maturity is reached between two and six years of age, and cutts often spawn only once, sometimes surviving to become ten

Perhaps the most difficult aspect of fishing for cutthroat trout is actually locating the fish in the brackish estuaries that they love. This means you must search out certain types of structure. Look for areas in the estuary that have both shallow and deep weed lines – these are always prime feeding spots for cutts. Also concentrate on submerged and decaying logs that are favorite hiding places for cutthroat while they are waiting for passing prey. Other special locations are rocky humps, submerged stream beds, and adjacent dropoffs, especially when these are populated by schools of minnows. Remember, location is the key!

SCOTT RIPLEY

years of age. Food in the ocean consists of sand lance, shrimp, and various fishes. Many cutthroat do not migrate to sea and inhabit various streams, rivers, and lakes, feeding on both aquatic and terrestrial insects such as midges, mayflies, caddis flies, and beetles. Small fishes such as trout, sculpin, and stickleback are eaten as well. Their diet also includes planktonic crustaceans, crayfish, salmon eggs, and even dead salmon. Cutthroat do not compete well with other species, especially the rainbow trout, which have made serious incursions on many native cutthroat populations. Although cutthroat will take prey from the water's surface or mid-depths, they prefer bottom feeding. They are not known for their intelligence or wariness and are therefore very vulnerable to overfishing. This, in turn, has frequently led to catch-and-release regulations on numerous cutthroat streams.

FISHING TACKLE Cutthroat are taken by spinning, bait-fishing, and fly-fishing. For inland streams, rivers, and lakes, an ultra-light or light- to medium-action rod and reel combination is often used to cast or troll small spoons, plugs, or spinners. Almost any lure that is small enough to cast effectively with 6- or 8-pound-test line will be effective as long as it can be presented close to the bottom. The retrieve should be medium to fast, with occasional pauses. Bait-fishermen should use worms, crayfish, and minnows fished on or near the bottom. Fly-anglers employ streamers, wet flies, and nymphs that can be presented near the bottom. Attractor-fly color patterns often include yellow and orange, and Wooly Worm flies, especially in brown or green, are very popular.

FISHING TECHNIQUES Since cutts are bottom feeders, wobbling plugs and

SCOTT RIPLEY

1 *Because cutthroat trout are so elusive, it is doubly important to fish every structural element or current break as thoroughly as possible.*

2 *When using bait for cutthroat trout, cut your line and leave the hook in a fish that has been deeply hooked. The stomach acids will dissolve the hook and not damage the fish. This is much safer than trying to remove a deeply imbedded hook and damaging the fish.*

3 *Giving cutthroat trout a choice of two lures can often*

bring results. Try tying on a 12-inch piece of monofilament to your spoon or spinner and attach a fly to ride behind your main lure. Sometimes it's only the trailing fly that these fish will hit.

4 *The tiny crankbaits that are so effective on cutthroat often need to be weighted with a couple of small split shot in*

order to get the lure diving down closer to feeding fish.

5 *A Polaroid camera is an inexpensive way to preserve your memories when fishing for gorgeous cutthroat trout. They're easy to use, you can see the immediate results of your photographic efforts, and you can release the fish to fight another day.*

spoons should be cast, trolled, or jigged along rocky bottoms and especially near dropoffs. Cutthroat also frequent slow-moving waters near brush, stumps, or larger boulders. They can be very shy. The angler should use light lines and small spinning lures as well as a reasonably stealthy approach in both lakes and streams. The best fishing periods are undoubtedly during the early morning and the late evening.

Fly-fishermen look for cutthroat fishing in both fresh and salt water. In fresh water, the best fly-fishing occurs when large numbers of mayflies hatch, often from July to September. They are also found in the deeper and cooler waters of lakes. In spring and early summer, fly-anglers will fish in shallow saltwater areas near river mouths, along with spin-fishermen and bait-anglers. The ebb periods of the tides, when entire schools of cutthroat often appear, are generally the best times, and the angling can be unforgettable. Flies that imitate shrimp or other oceangoing bait fish are preferred, and constructions with lively, undulating actions are often the most successful. Although the cutt is a vigorous fighter, it is not known for dazzling acrobatics, but will typically run and twist when hooked.

Dolly Varden

J. REIST

DOLLY VARDEN
CHAR ARE
NORMALLY MUCH
LIGHTER IN
COLOR THAN
ARCTIC CHAR.

COMMON NAMES brook trout, Dolly Varden, Dolly Varden char, red-spotted trout or char, sea trout

DESCRIPTION Although the Dolly Varden can sometimes exhibit strikingly beautiful colors, this member of the char family has often been maligned as an unwanted predator by many anglers. In fact, it was so disliked that it actually had a bounty placed on it at one time in hopes of its eradication. The Dolly Varden can, however, be classed as a game fish in every sense of the term. It is particularly sought after in the headwaters of its habitat, where it is considered a very spunky quarry indeed. It also plays a sporting role when other more popular game fish like trout and salmon are not available.

The Dolly Varden is very close in appearance to the Arctic char and at one time was thought to be only a subspecies of the Arctic char instead of a distinct species. The Dolly Varden is trout-like in appearance, with an elongated muscular body. Its coloring can vary dramatically. Sea-run fish have dark blue backs with bright silvery sides fading to a white belly. Freshwater fish are olive to dark brown on their backs with the sides being a pale variation of the back. The back and upper sides of the fish are characterized by numerous yellow, orange, or red markings that are usually smaller than that of the Arctic char (often smaller than the pupil of the eye of the fish). When spawning in fresh water, this fish can turn a magnificent red on its sides, making it quite striking.

SIZE The Dolly Varden is generally smaller than the closely related Arctic char. The average catch for an angler is between 2 and 5 pounds. The world record stands at

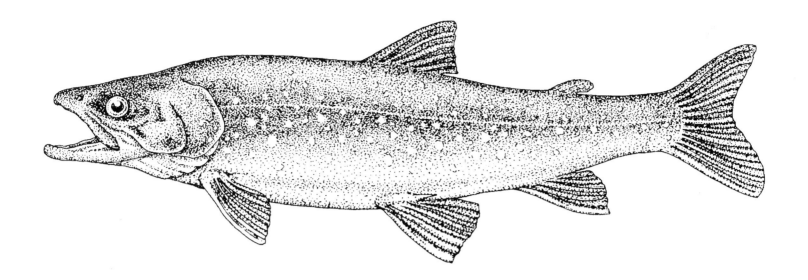

a whopping 32 pounds, although catching a Dolly Varden over 10 pounds is considered unusual. Size often depends upon location. Fish living in areas of high altitudes rarely grow to more than a few pounds. Sea-run fish really put on the beef after about three to four years, when their diet changes from insects to other fishes. They can be voracious predators, feeding on any type of fish – bait fish or small game fish like trout and salmon smolts.

DISTRIBUTION The Dolly Varden is widely distributed along the west coast of North America in salt and fresh water. Their most southerly range reaches to the streams of northern California, and their distribution extends all the way up to Alaska. In Canada, isolated populations may be found as far east as the South Saskatchewan River. The inland regions harbor nonanadromous populations, while the coastal regions feature anadromous and nonanadromous varieties.

BEHAVIOR AND HABITAT Small Dolly Varden feed on a variety of plankton and insects through their first few years of development. Smaller stream fish feed on a variety of insects, snails, leeches, and, in the fall, salmon eggs, turning to other fishes as they grow in size. The Dolly Varden char's undesirable image stems from its rapacious

SPECIAL TIP

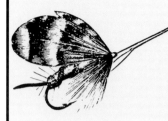

The spinning-tackle enthusiast who seeks consistent success with Dolly Varden should learn a few tricks from the fly-angler. Spin-fishermen often cast a variety of spoons and spinners for Dolly Varden, but the best fishing occurs in late September when Dollies are feeding heavily on salmon eggs. This means split-shot and salmon-egg flies, even for the spin angler. The remarkable success will be just reward for this switch in tactics.

THE SEA-RUN DOLLY VARDEN ENTER FRESH-WATER RIVERS ONLY TO SPAWN.

hunger as it grows larger, causing it to feed on the smolts of various salmon and steelhead species. Studies performed on anadromous strains of Dolly Varden have found that salmon make up only a small percentage of their diet.

For the first three to four years, small Dolly Varden remain in their native streams. Afterward, the anadromous variety moves to coastal waters, but never too far from the river mouths. Often, in fact, they will remain in the tidal waters, returning to freshwater streams and rivers in late summer.

FISHING TACKLE Dolly Varden can be taken using a variety of spinning and fly-casting tackle. Lures for the spin-angler often vary, ranging from between a selection of small spinners and tiny spoons for resident stream fish to larger spinners, spoons, and crankbaits for fish feeding on minnows and other fishes. When pursuing Dolly Varden, the angler has to decide on the relative size of tackle to use, depending on the size of the fish. Anglers seeking larger fish will use medium-size outfits with 10-pound-test line instead of the medium-light outfits, with 6- to 8-pound-test line, that are used for the smaller fish.

Fly-fishing is one of the most popular methods of tangling with this northern beauty. Dollies will regularly take wet flies and streamers presented with a 6/7-weight outfit. The keen fly-angler can succeed with a delicately presented dry fly.

QUICK TIPS

NORM WALLACHY

1 *Fall fishing for Dolly Varden often involves the use of salmon roe. Anglers using this method will do well to use a float to register light takers.*

2 *The spin-angler can take a tip from the fly-fisher by matching the hatch when Dolly Varden are feeding heavily on nymphs. Simply tie on the proper fly and clamp on some split shot partway up the line to delicately cast with this presentation.*

3 *Even though the fishing action may be hot, always approach a potential holding spot on a river from* *downstream. In this way, you ensure that you don't spook the very biggest and often wariest fish.*

4 *When the fishing slows down, tie on a bright piece of* *yarn above your lure to function as an attractor.*

5 *Use flashy flies and lures with erratic action for the most consistent Dolly Varden success.*

FISHING TECHNIQUES Fishing techniques for spin-fishermen often involve casting a variety of artificial lures for Dolly Varden. The light-tackle enthusiast will seek the many pools or deep runs when the fish are in their stream habitat. Bottom-bouncing a spinner often produces bone jarring strikes in the cold, clear inland streams where these fish are feisty and ready to smash your offering. Casting spoons that imitate the various bait fish are the most productive in estuaries. No matter what your pleasure, fly or spinning gear, casting along current breaks and eddies will consistently produce results.

Inconnu

ROYAL COACHMAN LODGE

THE "SHEEFISH"
IS ONE OF THE
SLICKEST-LOOK-
ING SPECIES.

COMMON NAMES connie, conny, inconnu, sheefish

DESCRIPTION Thanks to its large size and its distribution in remote areas, the inconnu has attained more of a mystique as a game fish than any other Canadian member of the whitefish family, as suggested by its French name "inconnu," which means "unknown." Connies are a fish of the far north. They migrate into rivers in late summer and fall, much like salmon. And, like many salmon, they often achieve a large size and fighting prowess that add much to their appeal.

Inconnu are silvery-colored whitefishes, with green to pale brown backs. Their dorsal and caudal fins are tipped with dark pigments, with the other fins usually clear. Their heads are long, broad, and shallow, and their mouths are large, with the lower jaw projecting beyond the upper.

SIZE Inconnu grow to a larger size than any of the other whitefishes. Most fish caught by anglers range from 18 to 30 inches in length and weigh from 6 to 12 pounds. Sport anglers in Alaska and the Northwest Territories commonly catch connies of 20 pounds or more. The largest known fish from the Great Slave Lake drainage system was a 55-pound monster and was caught around 1943 in Big Buffalo River. One weighing just over 63 pounds was also reported caught by Mr. K. H. Lang at the mouth of the Mackenzie River on July 12, 1936. More recently, a 54.7-pound connie was caught in Great Slave Lake.

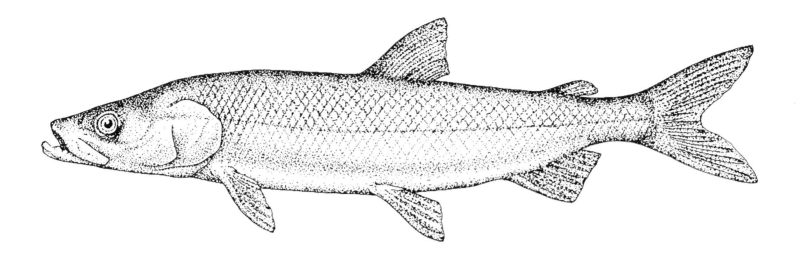

DISTRIBUTION Inconnu are found in northwestern North America and in the Arctic drainages of northern Asia to the White Sea. Connies also occur in the northern Caspian Sea and its drainages.

In North America, this species is found from the Kuskokwim River in the Bering Sea (Alaska) north to the Anderson River near Cape Bathurst, N.W.T. They also occur in many parts of the Yukon River systems, and in the southern Yukon and in northern British Columbia, notably the Liard River system.

BEHAVIOR AND HABITAT The food of freshwater populations of inconnu in Great Slave Lake consists mainly of small fishes, mostly other small whitefishes, but also northern pike, nine-spine sticklebacks, goldeye, minnows, Arctic lamprey, and some small inconnu. Inconnu in the Yukon River are even known to eat immature chinook salmon.

Young inconnu eat aquatic insect larvae and planktonic crustaceans. They change from an invertebrate diet in rivers to a fish diet upon entering large water systems such as Great Slave Lake and after reaching adulthood at about four years of age when they switch to a diet of fish.

Inconnu have both resident freshwater and anadromous life histories. Little is known about the ocean life of this species. Inconnu in lakes migrate up tributary streams

THE DEEP, COLD
LAKES OF THE
YUKON PRODUCE
GOOD CATCHES
OF INCONNU.

S P E C I A L   T I P

Inconnu can be caught with tactics similar to those used for trout. They are particularly attracted to wobbling plugs, spinners, and spoons. There are a few tricks to increase the action of these lures in slower waters. Many wobbling plugs such as the Rapala Count-down can be enhanced with a split ring inserted through the eye. All spoons should be fished with a snap swivel. Spinners can be fished without swivels, which will increase their action at slower speeds. This last spinner tactic, how-ever, will cause your line to be-come twisted. To correct the problem, simply tie on the spoon and snap swivel combo for a while and let the swivel straighten your line again.

in summer to spawn, and move back to lakes in late fall.

It's suspected that inconnu spawn only once every two, three, or four years. Spawning fish lay from 125,000 to 325,000 eggs. In the Big Buffalo River, young inconnu re-main for at least two years before descending to Great Slave Lake, al-though this pattern may not be typ-ical for all waters.

Many anglers in the Great Slave Lake drainage system concentrate their efforts for connies on tributary rivers. The largest runs occur in Big Buffalo and Taltson rivers, with lesser runs reported in Slave, Little Buffalo, and Hay rivers. The up-stream spawning migrations of this fish are often protracted, offering many chances for anglers. However, connies are said to be most vulner-able to anglers on their downstream migrations. This is when they head back toward the wintering lakes, and when they begin to accelerate their feeding on small fish.

FISHING TACKLE Since larger inconnu are fish eaters, spoons, spinners, and jigs are effective baits. Krocodiles,

1 *Inconnu are much more active on overcast days. Concentrate your angling on these days for the most consistent success.*

2 *Hot-spots for inconnu are locations where two streams or rivers join together. A normal river flowing into a glacial river is a prime location.*

3 *One of the best ways to locate active inconnu is to look for rolling fish on the surface, so keep your eyes peeled for* good catches.

4 *Because inconnu are known to jump several times during a fight, make sure your hooks are razor sharp and set the hook several times to ensure adequate hook penetration.*

5 *Inconnu will often feed on migrating salmon fingerlings. At this time, fly-anglers will use flies that match the size and look of the fingerlings. Surprisingly, tarpon flies work well in this situation.*

Pixies, Mepps, and Mister Twisters are some of the favorite brandnames of lures used by guides in Alaska and the Northwest Territories.

Casting and jigging rods capable of handling 10- to 20-pound fish are standard. Reels should be spooled with at least 12-pound test for the main line.

Connies are also attracting a growing number of fly-fishers seeking a novel quarry in remote locations. Fairly stiff 9-weight rods are needed for inconnu, especially in the larger spawning rivers. Streamers and any fair-sized minnow-imitation pattern are good starting-points for flies.

FISHING TECHNIQUES Connies can be jigged in lakes much like lake trout, but the majority of guides for inconnu pursue anadromous populations of this fish in large coastal rivers in Alaska and the Northwest Territories. Clients typically fly into main camps, then find the migratory schools of inconnu by using jet boats. Once a school of rolling fish is located, anglers cast spoons, spinners, or flies to the milling fish, and the action can be hectic.

Kokanee

COMMON NAMES Kennerly's salmon, kickininee, kokanee, landlocked sockeye, okiedokie salmon, silver trout

DESCRIPTION The kokanee and sockeye salmon are the same species, *Oncorhynchus nerka*. The main dif-

A NICE PAIR OF SILVER, LAKE-CAUGHT KOKANEE.

R. BRUNT

ference is that sockeye grow in salt water and kokanee grow in fresh water. Kokanee look similar to their sea-run brethren in most aspects except size; sockeye tend to grow larger in the richer marine environment. Wherever they grow, this species has the reddest and tastiest flesh of all the salmon in North America, making it a highly prized game fish.

The kokanee is a long and streamlined salmon. Its head is pointed, it has a small dorsal fin, and its color is generally silvery during the summer, turning to hues of red and green when it is ready to spawn.

SIZE Kokanee grow fairly rapidly, especially in their first year. Fish introduced to Boulter Lake in Ontario, for example, grew to 5.5 inches in their first year. Populations of kokanee in northern British Columbia lakes usually mature at 8 to 9 inches, while those in the southern parts of the province reach 12 to 15 inches. Larger kokanee are caught each year, with fish up to 8 pounds reported.

DISTRIBUTION The kokanee is found over most of the range of the sockeye, which includes watersheds from the Klamath River in California, north to Point Hope, Alaska. This species is also found in Asia from northern

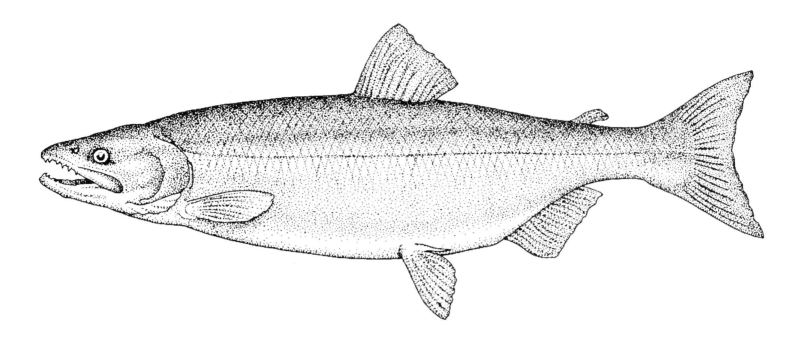

Hokkaido, Japan, to the Anadyr River, U.S.S.R.

The kokanee occurs naturally in Alaska, the Yukon, British Columbia, Washington, Idaho, and Oregon. Kokanee have also been introduced widely in North America. In the United States populations are found in Maine, California, Montana, Colorado, Connecticut, New York, Pennsylvania, Vermont, North Dakota, Nevada, Utah, and Wyoming. In Canada they are found in Alberta, Saskatchewan, Manitoba, and Ontario. Kokanee have also been introduced into lakes Huron, Michigan, Superior, and Ontario, although the Lake Ontario introduction failed.

BEHAVIOR AND HABITAT Kokanee feed mainly on pelagic plankton, primarily euphausids and other shrimp-like animals. They also eat bottom organisms, water mites, mayflies, and other terrestrial insects.

Kokanee spawn in the fall, mainly in September and October in Kootenay Lake as well as in other kokanee-stocked lakes in British Columbia. They spawn slightly

later in November and December in some areas of Ontario. Spawning in other areas may occur from August to February, in 1 to 30 feet of water.

Kokanee generally mature, spawn, and die at four years of age, but some spawn as young as two,

"WEDDING BAND" SPINNERS ARE VERY POPULAR RIGS ON THE WEST COAST.

1 When trolling river inlets for kokanee, it sometimes helps to use planer boards to take your lure out away from the boat. This is particularly useful on bright days in super-clear water conditions.

2 When fishing for kokanee in dirty water, try using a rattling crankbait to help the fish home in on your lure. A vibrating spinner like the Blue Fox Vibrax is also a top choice in dirty-water conditions.

3 Think small when it comes to lure selection for kokanee. Too many anglers use big artificial lures that simply intimidate these insect- and plankton-eating fish.

4 Concentrate your angling efforts just after ice-out for aggressively feeding kokanee salmon.

5 Jigging with a tear-drop jig gives a very effective presentation to imitate the invertebrate type of food that makes up the bulk of a kokanee's diet.

and others, as old as eight years of age. The colored adults usually spawn in tributary rivers of lakes, though some will choose gravel beds along lake shores. Numbers of eggs vary with the size of the female, usually ranging between 350 and 1,750 eggs, with an average of 450. In B.C., eggs hatch from December through January, with fry emerging from March through May.

During the summer, kokanee are found in schools at all depths in lakes, although they are most concentrated in the upper-middle layers. They move to deeper water in summer and winter.

FISHING TACKLE Since kokanee are plankton feeders, many anglers unfamiliar with this species think that they are difficult fish to catch. The trick is to use proper tackle and to find the location of the fish. Locating schools of kokanee is made easier with fish finders, and trolling is the standard method of catching them. Since kokanee may be in deep water, most trollers use deep-diving planers or downriggers to get their lures down to the strike zone.

Spinners will often fool river-running kokanee. There are several ways to present a spinner, depending on how the fish are hitting. If the fish are active and aggressive, the angler can toss his spinner upstream and retrieve it relatively quickly with the current. If the fish are holding in the centers of the pools, it is best to cast the spinner upstream at a 45-degree angle and retrieve it much more slowly past the fish. To cover the tail sections of the pools, the spinner should be cast straight across the current near the middle of the pool. It is then allowed to "hover" and remains almost stationary in the water until the current causes it to "arc" across the end of the pool.

Small flashers, tinsel trains, and gang trolls are often used by anglers to attract the kokanee. Willow-leaf trolls are fairly standard fare on Kootenay and other British Columbia lakes. Wedding Band spinners are a very popular west coast lure for kokanee, but a variety of small spinners also work, including homemade rigs of small red beads together with a small spinner blade. Some anglers will even add a kernel of corn to this whole contraption. Others will replace the spinners with small hooks baited with worms, salmon eggs, and other baits.

FISHING TECHNIQUES Since kokanee are generally small, many anglers troll with small rods to increase the quality of the fight, and 6- to 7-foot lengths are standard. Anglers familiar with trolling techniques for any of the large salmon will have little trouble adjusting their techniques for kokanee. Good-quality fish finders, with the high resolution needed to see smaller fish, can reduce frustration and greatly improve catches. Fish finders also help to track the seasonal migration of kokanee to spawning areas, as well as their vertical movements in lakes.

Terminal tackle is trolled anywhere from 30 to 60 yards behind the boat; line lengths should be increased for every corresponding increase in light intensity and water clarity. Anglers may also want to experiment, especially if kokanee seem spooky, and troll their various lures and bait without attractors of any kind. A slow trolling speed of one mile per hour is standard.

Lake Trout

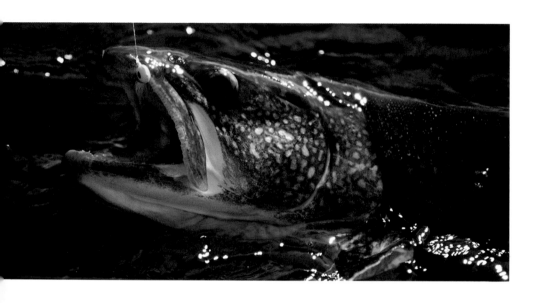

JIGS HAVE
BECOME
CONSISTENT
PRODUCERS OF
LAKE TROUT.

COMMON NAMES great grey trout, Great Lakes char, Great Lakes trout, grey trout, laker, lake trout, landlocked salmon, Mackinan trout, mountain trout, namaycush, salmon trout, taque, togue

DESCRIPTION More than any other species, the lake trout deserves the title of Canada's "northern" game fish. It is a perfectly adapted inhabitant of the clear, cool, deep lakes of Canada's north. Although it possesses a characteristically trout-like form, the laker actually belongs to the char clan, along with the brook trout, the Arctic char, and the Dolly Varden. Lakers also possess a rather large head, with large eyes and fins and a deeply forked tail. The typical laker has a gray-green to gray-blue back, with numerous whitish spots along the sides and a cream-colored belly. In some lakes the lakers have no spots at all and are an overall silvery color.

SIZE Lake trout are known to grow to gigantic proportions, which invariably draws the keen attention of the angling community. They are believed to be able to survive for forty to fifty years, which, in part, accounts for their great size. Although most lakers caught by anglers are in the 10-pound class, many lunkers of 20 to 30 pounds have also been caught, especially in the Northwest Territories, particularly in Great Bear Lake and Great Slave Lake. In fact, Great Bear Lake easily dominates the various line-class records of the International Game Fish Association, owning six of the total of nine available world records. Great Bear Lake also boasts the all-tackle world-record lake trout, which was

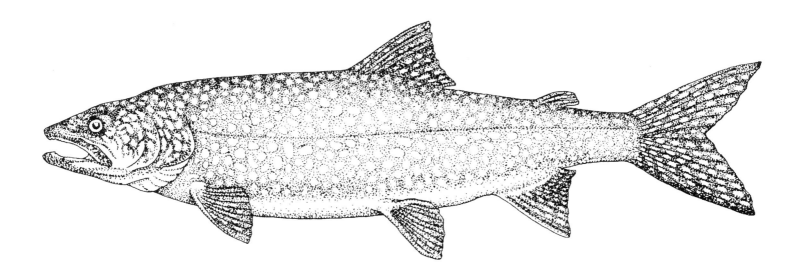

taken in 1991 and weighed 66.5 pounds. Canada is so well known, in fact, for its huge lakers that it has become a mecca for trophy anglers. The largest known lake trout was taken in a commercial gill net in 1961 in Lake Athabaska and weighed a full 102 pounds. This colossus was a sexual oddity, however, completely lacking gonads and unable to spawn. It became a relentless feeding machine and eventually attained a girth of 44 inches and a length of 50 inches, giving it a remarkably obese appearance.

DISTRIBUTION The lake trout occurs over most of Canada, including western Nova Scotia, New Brunswick, Quebec, and most of Ontario. Lakers are also common in the more northerly portions of Manitoba, Saskatchewan, Alberta, and British Columbia. They have become abundant in the Yukon, the Northwest Territories, and many of the Arctic islands. In the United States, the lake trout is far less common and is found in the New England states, some of the Great Lakes states, and a few

western states, where recently introduced populations are gradually becoming established.

BEHAVIOR AND HABITAT Much knowledge has been gathered about Canada's premier game fish. Although lakers spawn some time in

If you're trolling and marking fish on your sonar but are not able to register a strike, special tactics are required. Troll over the spot, moving the boat in an "S" pattern, which causes the lure to hesitate, tumble downward, and speed up again in an enticing "fluttering" fashion. If you're using a downrigger, crank the cannonball up and down so the lure flutters irresistibly upward and downward.

the autumn, timing varies according to differences in geography, seasons, and weather. In most areas, lakers will spawn in October, usually on rocky shoals in lakes. Spawning occurs at night, with the eggs deposited into crevices between large rocks. A large female may deposit between 10,000 and 20,000 eggs, which incubate in their sheltered crevices for several months before they hatch. Sexual maturity is reached by age seven and sometimes even later in slower-growing specimens in northern environments. Lake trout prefer deep, clear lakes especially in the more southern portions of their range, although they are also common in more shallow lakes and rivers in the far north. Lake trout prefer to spawn in the shallows in autumn and then disperse throughout the lake at all depths during winter. With the arrival of spring, lake trout are commonly found in the water's upper layers, especially immediately after ice thaws. As spring advances, lakers retreat to deeper waters. They spend the summer months at cooler depths below the thermocline, which is the border between the warmer surface layer and the cooler bottom layers of a lake. Lakers are very successful predators and feed upon crustaceans, aquatic and terrestrial insects, numerous fish species, and, occasionally, small mammals. Their fish diet includes whitefish, smelt, perch, sculpins, emerald shiners, longnose suckers, and especially ciscoes. Lakers will, however, adjust their diet according to the type of forage available. In northern Quebec, near Ungava Bay, lakers were often found to have both mice and shrews in their stomachs.

FISHING TACKLE Lake-trout tackle is often fairly heavy. There is a long tradition in Canada of using heavy wire lines with special reels and short, stout rods. These awkward but effective outfits were necessary in order to place the lures at the great depths of 50 or even 100 feet that are frequented by lakers. Modern technology, however, has given anglers completely new equipment – the downrigger and the electronic sonar. The sonar's video screen shows the depth of the lakers, their

OPPOSITE:

A 33-POUND

LAKER FROM

SASKATCHEWAN.

bait fish, and the all-important thermocline. The downrigger, to which the trolling line is attached, then sends the lure down to the pre-set depth via a lead cannon ball attached to a wire cable. When a fish strikes the lure, a special release mechanism frees the line from the downrigger cable, allowing the angler to enjoy the unfettered battle of a large laker at 100 feet or more. There are many popular lake-trout trolling lures, including the traditional Williams Wabler, or the myriad special deep-trolling spoons such as the Flutterlite, the Sutton 31, or the Andy Reeker.

FISHING TECHNIQUES Lake trout are taken by many methods, including casting, bait-fishing, ice fishing, and especially by trolling, either with or without downriggers. The best time to cast for them is during the lake's ice thaw in early spring or in autumn prior to their spawning in the shallows. Anglers await them near points, shoals, dropoffs, and river mouths and use a variety of spinners, spoons, and plugs. Ice-fishing is usually conducted above known laker hangouts such as points, shoals, or weed beds that harbor bait fish. Holes are drilled with manual or gasoline-driven augers, and bait such as minnows are used with special "tip-up" devices. Other ice-fishermen use special rods to jig lures, such as the Jigging Rapala, the Pilkki, or the Swedish Pimple. Most lakers, however, are taken by trolling using numerous tactics. During spring and fall, the shorelines can be worked, even with light spinning tackle, by "flat lining" with body baits such as the Rebel or the Thinfin, or with spoons such as the West River or Little Cleo. In very shallow areas, anglers sometimes employ planer boards, which carry both line and lure off to one side so prospective lakers are not "spooked" by the boat. Deep trolling in depths of 30 to 60 feet is often conducted over shoals or other prominent underwater structures. Bait-fisherman often use large live or dead minnows, smelts, or herring, and this technique seems especially effective for taking very large lakers. Trolling speeds will vary from very slow to medium speeds.

JIM MARKOU

QUICK TIPS

1 At different times of the year, lakers are found only at certain depths. The best way to fish such specific depth ranges is to use the "float-jigging" technique. The line, tipped with a jig, is allowed to run through the center of the slip bobber until it hits a "bobber stop," which is attached on the line at the required depth. When the line is pulled up through the float, the jig dances under the water at precisely the right depth. When a laker picks up the lure, the float dives, telling the angler when to set the hook. This is a great rig!

2 When trolling for lakers at depths of 40 to 60 feet it's important to choose lure colors that will be visible to cruising fish. Fluorescent colors, such as orange, pink, and chartreuse, are the most visible at any depth. Natural colors, such as blue, green, and black, are also good. By rule of thumb, use fluorescent colors on overcast days and the naturals on bright, clear days.

3 One of the most effective rigs for lake-trout trolling is the spoon-fly combination. Simply remove the treble hook from your spoon and replace it with 12 inches of monofilament holding a flashy wet fly or streamer. The spoon attracts the fish from great distances, while the fly actually draws the strike.

4 The Christmas Tree or Gang Troll is one of the oldest and most popular lake-trout lures. It consists of a number of spinning blades and spoons rigged close together on a leader. To this gang troll is added some monofilament with a bait rig. The many flashing spinners and spoons resemble a school of bait fish and attract lakers from afar. The bait rig actually hooks the attacking lakers.

5 When lake trout are found only at great depths, the best way to catch them is with a downrigger. A less expensive and less complicated device for reaching these fish is the Dipsey Diver. This inexpensive device is attached to the trolling line and will move it away from the boat and down to a predetermined depth. Once a fish is hooked, the Dipsey Diver is "tripped" so that it does not offer much resistance in the water, enabling the angler to enjoy an unencumbered battle with the fish.

Largemouth Bass

COMMON NAMES bass, black bass, bucketmouth, green bass, largemouth, largemouth bass, largemouth black bass

DESCRIPTION The largemouth bass is pursued by countless thousands of sport fishermen throughout North America. Certainly it's the most valuable game fish on the continent in terms of cash stakes in the many popular bass tournament competitions. Millions of dollars are awarded annually to competitors for both quantity and size of fish caught. Bass tournament "pros" can actually rival their golf and tennis counterparts in terms of annual earnings.

The short, chunky body of a largemouth makes this muscular fish capable of quick bursts of speed along with phenomenal maneuverability when pursuing prey as an adult or when escaping from predators as an immature fingerling. The most striking physical feature of the largemouth bass is its massive mouth, hence the strange nickname "bucketmouth." Color patterns, varying from light to dark green to olive to black, create perfect camouflage to protect the young in the weeds and to assist in the unceasing hunt for prey.

SIZE Although the average largemouth bass caught by anglers weighs 1 to 2 pounds, this stocky and feisty fish provides a challenge, especially when it's caught in its usual and difficult environment of heavy weeds or woody cover. The current world-record bucketmouth was caught back in 1932 in Montgomery Lake in Georgia. It weighed in at 22 pounds, 4 ounces.

DISTRIBUTION The native Canadian range of the largemouth bass covers the lower Great Lakes and the associated water systems of southern Ontario and Quebec. In the United States, the central to lower parts of the Mississippi River and lower southeastern states are the largemouth's original range. Now, because of aggressive stocking programs, it can be found throughout the whole eastern portion of the United States in great numbers, and in many of the southern states, right across to California. In fact, there are at least

FOR A LARGE-MOUTH, THIS IS TRULY HEAVEN!

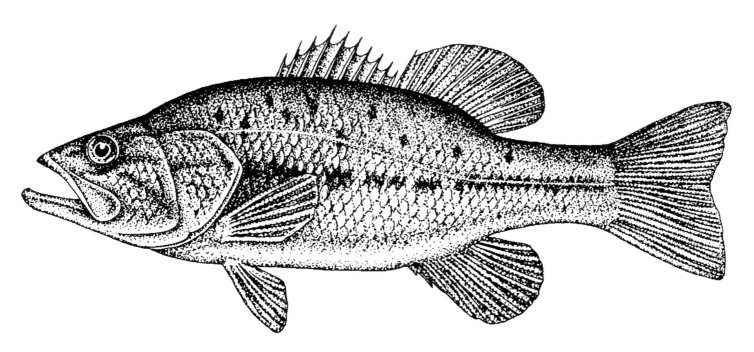

isolated pockets of largemouth in al-most every continental U.S. state. The whole of southern Ontario and much of Quebec hold thriving pop-ulations of fish, and there are even scattered pockets of bass in B.C., Al-berta, Saskatchewan, and Manitoba.

BEHAVIOR AND HABITAT Largemouth bass have earned quite an exagger-ated reputation for their ability to consume prey of large proportions. Indeed, the size of their yawning "maw" makes them able to swallow ducklings, snakes, and even the odd small muskrat. There is no question, however, that much of their prey consists of other fishes like min-nows, small perch, sunfish, and even members of their own species. This diet is supplemented, espe-cially for young bass under 5 inches, with a variety of aquatic insects, and also substantial numbers of crayfish.

Most of the largemouth's prey is found in the highly fertile, shallow weedy areas of lakes. Although largemouth-bass populations have been found in deep water, most of their feeding is in shallow water.

The easiest way to catch bass is

when they move into shallow water to look for prey. Here the angler has the best chance of tangling with old bucketmouth. Find an area of healthy weed growth in a warm-water lake or slow-moving river and, chances are, you'll catch a bass or two.

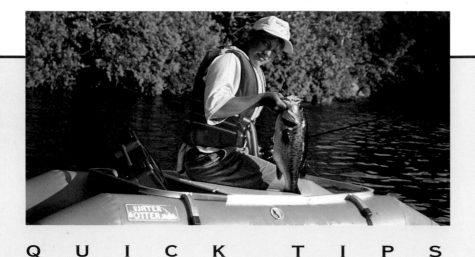

Q U I C K   T I P S

1 *Largemouth bass will often hit surface lures, even in the middle of the day. A weedless lure like a Breck's Timber Doodle or Heddon Moss Boss, worked across the lily pads and floating slop, will trigger strikes from aggressive or resting fish.*

2 *In very sparse weed cover, adding a trailer hook to your spinner bait or buzz bait can add a lot more fish to the boat that might otherwise not have been hooked. Always rig a trailer hook facing upwards to ensure that it's as weedfree as possible.*

3 *If you locate a really awesome-looking piece of cover like a downed tree, make sure you cast several times to it. Slowly work your weedless lure all around the cover because sometimes big fish take a while to be triggered into striking. The patience, though, is worth it.*

4 *When fishing surface lures for bass, always hesitate for a moment before setting the hook. Many anglers jump the gun and miss the fish because they set the hook too fast.*

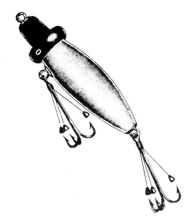

FISHING TACKLE No other species of game fish in the world has had such a wide variety of lures designed especially for it than the largemouth bass. Topwater lures like the Hula Popper and the Jitterbug have been popular for decades and have earned a treasured place in the bass fisherman's arsenal of tackle. Now they are complemented by sophisticated new lures like the "safety pin" spinner bait, for example, which is available in a multitude of colors and blade sizes. Add to this buzzbaits for aggressive fish and weedless spoons for especially heavy vegetation, and you have only a small part of the bass angler's arsenal. Plastic worms are the most popular lure because of their versatility, weedlessness, and big fish-catching ability.

With exotic colors like "tequila sunrise," "pumpkinseed," and "bubble gum," as well as standard colors like black, purple, and "motor oil," the simple plastic worm catches more bass every year than any other lure on the market.

Rods for catching bass are also varied but most are heavy duty in order to pull even medium-sized bass from the very dense weed cover in which they are often found. The line used for bass is also heavy duty for the same reason and often ranges from 10- to 20-pound-test breaking strength.

FISHING TECHNIQUES Although largemouth bass can be caught by trolling artificial lures and by casting live bait, certainly the most popular

way to fool big fish is by casting a variety of artificial lures. The consistently successful angler tries a variety of lures until the "hot" lure for the given weather and water conditions is found. Often, the angler will concentrate in prospective weedy or woody areas early in the morning and start by using fast-moving top-water lures for actively feeding and aggressive bass. If the fish are not willing to strike at these offerings, the angler should switch to a spinner bait. This lure can be retrieved at a variety of depths and speeds in order to entice wary bass, and it can be tossed into fairly heavy cover without tangling on weeds. If even spinnerbaits fail to produce, the angler will need to get even closer to the fish by tossing plastic worms or flipping jigs directly into the heavy weed cover. When bass are reluctant to strike all of these fast-moving lures, then a jig or worm is retrieved very slowly to give reluctant fish a better chance at devouring the angler's offering.

Bait-fishing for largemouth is popular in Florida where immense trophies are often taken in heavy underwater cover by using a balloon as a float with an 8- to 12-inch golden shiner as the bait. Live worms, crayfish, and 3- to 4-inch minnows are also very popular bait.

CRANKBAITS ARE DEADLY WHEN BASS ARE ACTIVE.

S P E C I A L T I P

When the fish aren't biting, slow down your presentation. This tactic is often overlooked even by the experienced pros. Often, the fish haven't moved away, but are simply inactive and not feeding aggressively. A slow-moving twister-tail jig or a worm trailed over a log or through the weeds can be tantalizing, even to a lethargic fish. Remember, presentation is the key to your success, so when the bait settles to the bottom, pause, twitch the bait with your rod tip, and then pause again throughout your retrieve.

Muskellunge

COMMON NAMES lunge, maskinonge, muskellunge, muskie, Wisconsin muskellunge

DESCRIPTION Few North American game fish have the ability to inflame the angler's imagination as much as the mighty muskellunge. Indeed, few other game fish can eclipse the muskie in size. Among all of the fierce predators of lakes and rivers, the muskellunge certainly reigns supreme. Lively tales of its attacks on people have not been documented but have added to its savage reputation.

The muskellunge has a long, torpedo-shaped, muscular body, the perfect shape for producing great bursts of speed when attacking prey. The differences between what were thought to be three subspecies have generally been only variations in coloring. Often, the muskellunge/pike hybrid or tiger muskellunge, which has very prominent vertical bars and spotting, has been confused with some highly marked purebred muskellunge.

SIZE The world record for muskellunge stands at 69 pound, 15 ounces. This behemoth was caught in 1957 in the St. Lawrence River and was an incredible 64.5 inches in length. Muskellunge are one of the fastest-growing freshwater game fish. In the first six months of their life they attain an average length of about 10 or 12 inches. Some very large Canadian muskellunge have been caught in recent years in the Moon River and Georgian Bay, and the world-record fish may soon be topped.

THE 65-POUND CANADIAN-RECORD MUSKIE CAUGHT IN 1988 BY KEN O'BRIEN IN GEORGIAN BAY.

JOHN POWER

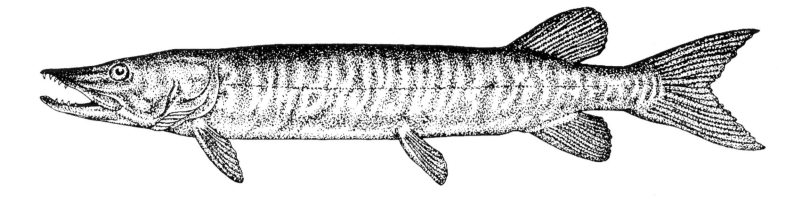

The average size of a muskellunge is between 10 and 20 pounds, but numerous fish weighing more than 30 pounds are caught from Canadian and American waters.

The tiger muskellunge exhibits what is known as "hybrid vigor" in its growth rate. Although, it doesn't quite attain the length of the true muskellunge, it certainly grows faster and is often a much heavier fish for its size. It also provides much more sport than the northern pike, making it a more desirable game fish.

DISTRIBUTION The muskellunge is native to the fresh waters of eastern North America. In Canada, it is found in Ontario and Quebec, and in a small area of water in southeastern Manitoba. It is also native to the lower Great Lakes and the St. Lawrence River along with its tributaries. In the United States, the muskie is found from the St. Lawrence River south to Tennessee and through Illinois into Wisconsin and Minnesota. It is native to parts of the Mississippi and the Ohio drainage systems.

In Canada, the tiger muskellunge has a somewhat limited range in those waters harboring both the muskellunge and the northern pike.

BEHAVIOR AND HABITAT Muskellunge are renowned for their ferocious strikes at prey such as unsuspecting

Muskies can be caught throughout the season, using a variety of fishing techniques. However, the best time to hook the highest number of fish relatively close to shore is during the fall. Muskies will feed heavily right up until "ice-up." Therefore, during these cold weather months, they will be located at the openings of bays, along steep dropping shorelines, and especially near rocky points. The most productive method of catching muskies under these conditions is by casting large plugs and, in particular, "jerk baits" in these areas.

walleye or sometimes even ducklings swimming on the surface. The muskellunge uses its great speed to suddenly burst upon its prey, often engulfing it in one devastating and swift bite. If their meal does not go down during the first gulp, then they will often hold the prey in their jaws and return to their lair to consume it. The main forage of adult muskellunge consists of perch, walleye, suckers, large minnows, and other fishes. Ducks, muskrats, squirrels, and snakes have all been consumed with relish by the larger specimens.

Muskellunge are solitary predators. They move very little, and once they have claimed a particular area in a lake, they will often drive other game fish away. Anglers who have had a strike from a muskie will carefully note the location and return to work the area repeatedly.

The muskellunge's habitat is varied. In shallow, weedy eutrophic lakes, they will often frequent areas adjacent to deep weed cover or sit near structures such as wood or rock piles. In clearer, deeper lakes, they are commonly found near deep weed lines, but will also set up their lairs close to steep dropoffs and fast-tapering shoals. Any of these types of locations that also have a good supply of forage will likely harbor sizable muskellunge.

FISHING TACKLE Because muskellunge grow to such great size, the tackle required to successfully catch these freshwater tigers is relatively "beefy." Stout rods with 17- to 30-pound-test line are the rule for this type of fishing. There are variations, however, in the type of tackle chosen. Anglers who choose to cast spinners will use only medium-heavy- to heavy-action rods while those using jerk baits often require special "pool cues," as superheavy rods are known. In most cases rods for taking muskellunge have extra long butts to allow two-handed casting of large, heavy lures and to make it easier to fight the fish.

Top lures for muskellunge are almost always quite sizable. Large

bucktail spinners are extremely effective, as well as the various oversized spinner baits. A variety of large crankbaits, plugs, and spoons are also quite useful when casting or trolling. The lure that is almost synonymous with the muskellunge is the so-called jerk bait. This type of lure is the most exciting lure to use for muskellunge because it is retrieved on or near the surface, and, when a muskie strikes this plug, the results are nothing short of heartstopping. And, of course, as with all muskellunge fishing, strong wire leaders are a must.

FISHING TECHNIQUES There are many angling methods for catching muskie, including casting, trolling, and live-bait fishing. In the late spring and early summer, muskies will often linger in the shallows after their spawning activities. Casting with spinners and spinner baits is often productive for catching aggressive fish as they feed after spawning. As summer progresses, many of these fish will drop into deeper-water haunts. During midsummer, when fishing in large,

deep, open-water lakes and large rivers, trolling large plugs becomes one of the most consistent ways to catch medium- to large-sized muskies. Often a depth finder helps in locating deep structures like rock piles, steep dropoffs, the underwater points of islands, and the deep edges of weed lines. Trolling through these prime areas often leads to success.

As summer progresses into fall, and muskellunge start feeding for the winter, they will often move to the shallows again, especially in rivers and smaller lakes. This is prime time for jerk baiting. A jerk bait is a fairly lifeless looking piece of wood, often similar to a section of hockey stick. It is, however, very effective in attracting big muskies. Most anglers toss it out to rock piles, shoals, and weed lines to coax resident muskellunge into striking. The lure is often jerked back to the boat so that it dives just under the surface. As it starts to float up toward the surface, the angler jerks the lure again to make it swim erratically like a wounded or sick bait fish — the perfect prey for the solitary feeding muskie.

BIG MUSKIES REQUIRE HEAVY GEAR.

Perch

and the sauger. It has a fairly elongated body, with two clearly separated dorsal fins, and its coloration is usually olive and yellow with orange fins. Six to eight darker vertical bands extend from its back and gradually fade near the belly.

The white perch belongs to the family *Percichthyidae* and is a relative of the striped bass and the giant sea basses. It has a much chunkier body shape than the yellow perch, and its coloration varies from olive on its back to silver green on its sides, terminating in a white belly. It has no bands, and its two dorsal fins are not separate.

SIZE Yellow perch usually weigh between 1/4 and 3/4 of a pound, although the larger lakes will frequently produce "jumbos" of 1 to 2 pounds. Schools of perch usually consist of fish of similar size, although one wonders if the 4-pound, 3-ounce world-record "yellow" that was caught in the Delaware River in New Jersey was traveling in such a school of abnormally large fish.

White perch average 8 to 10 inches in length and weigh a pound

JIM KOZMIK

PERCH LOVE
TO HOLD IN
SCHOOLS.

COMMON NAMES Yellow perch: American perch, coon perch, jack perch, lake perch, ringed perch, striped perch

White perch: little white bass, narrow-mouthed bass, silver perch

DESCRIPTION The yellow perch is a member of the family *Percidae*, and its closest relatives are the walleye

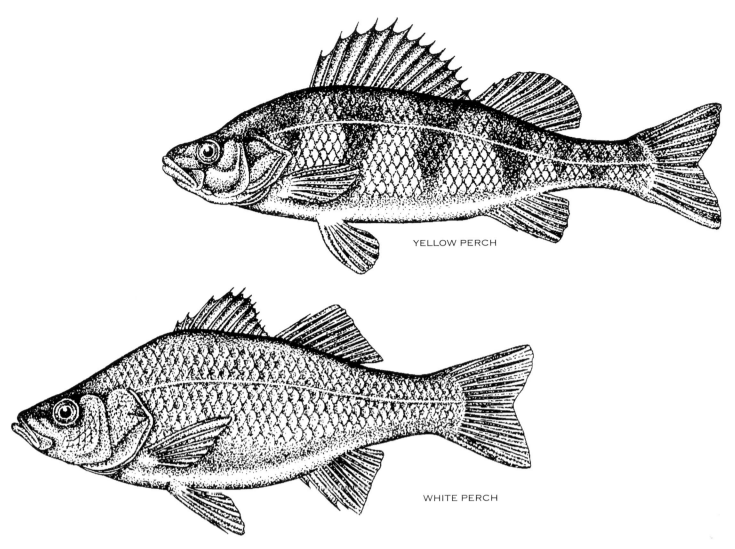

YELLOW PERCH

WHITE PERCH

or less, although some particularly fertile environments may produce larger fish of 2 or more pounds. The world angling record was set back in 1949 in Messalonskee Lake and the catch strained the weigh scales at 4 pounds, 12 ounces.

DISTRIBUTION Yellow perch have achieved a wide range in the fresh waters of the northern hemisphere. In the United States, this species is found along the east coast from Maine all the way to northern Florida and Alabama, and its range extends westward well past the Appalachian Mountains.

In Canada, the yellow perch has achieved a remarkable distribution including parts of Nova Scotia, New Brunswick, Quebec, Ontario,

Manitoba, Saskatchewan, Alberta, and even a small portion of British Columbia.

The white perch, although able to thrive in fresh water, seems to prefer brackish waters, and has a much more limited range, extending along the Atlantic coast of North America. In the United States, its range hugs the coastline in a narrow band from the St. Lawrence River to South Carolina. In Canada, it is found in limited areas of Prince Edward Island, Nova Scotia, and New Brunswick. White perch have even established themselves in Lake Ontario. They may soon become established in Lake Erie as well.

BEHAVIOR AND HABITAT Yellow perch flourish in both large and small lakes and are also at home in rivers. Ideal perch habitat consists of cool, clear water with a rock, gravel, or sand bottom and some vegetation. In those lakes with soft bottoms and massive weed beds that provide hiding places from predators, the perch are often very small as a result of high survival rates among the young.

Perch are not light sensitive like walleye and are generally not caught at night. Spawning takes place when water temperatures during spring reach 43 to 48 degrees Fahrenheit, usually at night and in weed, brush, or other cover, to which the ribbons of eggs will adhere. Yellow perch will remain in their spawning locations for a few weeks before moving into deeper water of 65 to 70 degrees Fahrenheit. In summer they are often found near the thermocline or the water layer where the temperature suddenly changes drastically. The thermocline is especially attractive to the fish when it occurs near bottom. They also haunt rocky shoals, islands, points, breakwaters, and bridge abutments, especially when the water reaches depths of 20 or more feet and the bottom is rocky or sandy with moderate vegetation. In fall and winter, yellow perch are found in more shallow water and offer a fishing bonanza for the ice-fisherman just before ice-out. They are not shy about feeding during the day when they pursue their prey with a keen visual sense, often cornering fish against a boulder or

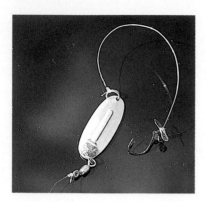

When the bait-fishing for perch is slow, it is often a good idea to add an attractor to your rig. Slide a colorful bead down your line above the hook. You can also tie a small spoon, minus its hook, on the line. Next add about 12 inches of lighter line where the hook used to be, and tie your hook on the other end. The spoon, when jigged, will attract perch to the bait below. In a pinch you can even twist a strip of aluminum foil around your line to create a primitive propeller.

other obstruction. Adult yellow perch will eat small fish, crustaceans, snails, leeches, and aquatic insects.

White perch are found in fresh, salt, or brackish water. Thus, they are taken by rod and reel in Atlantic coastal estuaries as well as in freshwater inland lakes. Spawning occurs in spring when water temperatures in tributary streams reach between 46 and 55 degrees Fahrenheit. White perch will swim in schools and seek out deeper water near shallow reefs, weed beds, and over-grown shorelines. In fall, the fish move into still deeper water of 30 feet or more. White perch will feed on aquatic insects, especially mayfly larvae, as well as small alewives, smelt, and other fish, including their own young. In winter, white perch become extremely lethargic and their food intake is sharply reduced.

FISHING TACKLE Lure fisherman can use almost their entire inventory of small, flashy lures for both yellow and white perch. Spinners such as the Toni, Mepps, or Panther Martin seldom fail. Likewise tiny spoons such as the Hopkins ST or the Williams Wabler. Small plugs such as the Flatfish or Lazy Ike are used occasionally also. Perch will eagerly attack ultra-light jigs as well as jig-spinner combinations of all kinds. The ice-fisherman is more restricted in his lure selection when fishing for yellow perch. He can choose between different tear-drop lures, such as the Fairy or the Speck, and jigging spoons, such as the Jig-A-Spoon, Swedish Pimple, and the Mr. Champ in sizes ranging from 1/16 to 1/8 ounces.

FISHING TECHNIQUES Yellow perch are a schooling fish. Anglers who begin to catch smaller fish usually move to search for a school of larger perch. Bait-fishermen routinely employ No. 4 or 6 hooks baited with worms, leeches, small minnows, or even thin shreds of fish meat. When the yellow perch are spawning, anglers suspend tiny minnows or insect larvae near fish-holding bottom structure. Reefs or rocky

1 *When using live minnows for perch, make sure they are tiny (no more than 2 inches long). Many anglers use larger minnows and never have more than a few hits in a day.*

2. *When ice-fishing for yellow perch, add a couple of dropper lines (where legal)*

to your main line. This will definitely increase your catch.

3 *Tipping a small jig or spinner with a worm can increase your chances of catching light-biting perch on those "off" days when the fishing is slow.*

4 *If you are out in a boat, taking in early-season yellow*

perch fishing, the most active fish will often be right beside the pack ice that is starting to break up.

5 *Early-spring hot-spots for yellow perch are shoals and rocky points, particularly when the sun is shining and warming these areas.*

dropoffs in 20 to 40 feet of water with moderate weed growth are often perch hot-spots. The fish are tempted with tiny, slowly retrieved jigs, spinners, and spoons, often baited with an elastic shred of fish meat.

White perch are easiest to catch during their annual spawning extravaganza when the industrious angler can catch them by the dozen. Worms are very effective, fished on bottom, dangling from a float, or trailing from the hook of a spoon or spinner. Small jigs, especially in

white or yellow patterns, are effective during the spawning period as well. Fly-anglers often enjoy sport with white perch, using yellow or white-red streamers. During the fall, white perch will stage false spawning runs along the same streams and rivers they used for spawning during the spring. During summer fish are often caught by trolling spinner-worm combinations, especially over rock points and reefs. When the fish are in deeper water, vertical jigging techniques are often successful.

SCIENTIFIC NAMES Chain pickerel: *Esox niger*
Redfin pickerel: *Esox americanus americanus*
Grass pickerel: *Esox americanus vermiculatus*

Pickerel

SUNSET — A
GREAT TIME TO
FISH FOR
PICKEREL.

COMMON NAMES black chain pike, duck-billed pike, eastern pickerel, grass pickerel, green pike, jack, lake pickerel, mud pickerel, pickerel, picquerelle, pike, reticulated pickerel, snake

DESCRIPTION Pickerel are members of the *Esocidae* (pike) family. Pickerel are not to be mistaken for walleye, which are often referred to in Ontario as pickerel. The walleye actually belongs to the perch family. Chain, redfin, and grass pickerels all have elongated bodies similar in appearance to that of the northern pike. The markings on the chain pickerel are easily distinguishable. As its name suggests, this fish has a series of chain-like marks running the length of its sides. The redfin pickerel usually has several vertical bars along its sides and amber to red-hued fins, after which it is named. The grass pickerel has similar vertical bars, but usually lacks the orange-red pigmentation in its fins.

SIZE The various pickerels are much smaller than the related northern pike and muskellunge. The grass pickerel is the smallest of the three, seldom growing to more than 10 inches in length. The largest specimen on record weighed less than 1 pound. The redfin pickerel grows slightly larger than the grass pickerel, attaining lengths of about 12 inches and qualifying it in the minds of anglers as a small though viable sport fish. The chain pickerel is the granddaddy of these pickerels, often attaining weights of 6 pounds or more. The largest chain pickerel on record to date weighed in at 9 pounds, 6 ounces. The average size, however, is between 15 and 18 inches, and most chain pickerels weigh slightly more than a pound.

DISTRIBUTION All three pickerels occur along the eastern part of North America and are restricted to fresh and only occasionally brackish water. The chain pickerel has a small range and is limited to a narrow band along the eastern seaboard from Nova Scotia down to the south-central part of Florida and then along the Gulf states to Texas and up the Mississippi drainage system. The redfin and grass pickerels

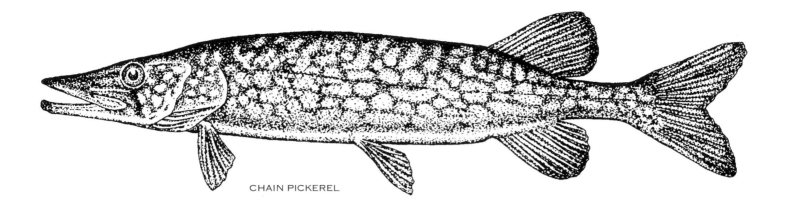

CHAIN PICKEREL

overlap in their range. They both occur in the St. Lawrence River and south along the eastern plains of the United States.

BEHAVIOR AND HABITAT Pickerels are known to be voracious feeders. They attack their prey with great speed and ferocity, especially for a fish of their size. The young of the species feed on small aquatic insects and, as these fish grow in size, they prey upon larger types of food. Adult fish feed mostly on minnows and other fishes as well as crayfish, tadpoles, and frogs. In fact, these fish will feed on anything that they can subdue, including the occasional mouse and snake. They often wait just inside the edge of heavy weed cover for unsuspecting prey to pass nearby, then rush out and seize their food. It should be noted that they are very reluctant to chase their prey into open water, preferring, instead, the sanctuary of weed growth. The chain, redfin, and grass pickerels will also feed under the ice during winter and thus provide sport for the ice-fishing community. All three pickerels spawn much like

the rest of the pike family. Spawning occurs mostly in the spring, although some fall spawning has been noted for all three species. They choose areas of vegetation along flooded stream banks or in the shallows of ponds and lakes. Soon after spawning, these fish move to the

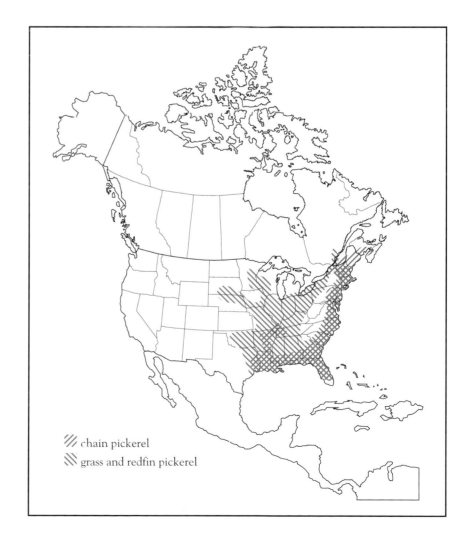

/// chain pickerel

\\\ grass and redfin pickerel

1 *Although members of the pickerel family may be small, you still have to handle them with care. After removing the hooks, even small fish should be gently cradled in the water until they have recovered enough to swim away on their own.*

2 *When fishing for pickerel in matted weeds, try a frog-imitating surface lure, especially on calm days. You can fish it right over the tops of weeds to get some of the biggest fish that are resting below.*

3 *Because pickerel are voracious feeders, start out retrieving your spoons or spinners quickly to stimulate aggressive strikes.*

4 *On slow days, when the fish are inactive, try suspending a 3- to 4-inch minnow, hooked through the back, below a bobber, along the edges of heavy weed growth. This is often the best way to get inactive fish to strike.*

5 *A good set of needle-nose pliers is a must, even for small pickerel. These fish can be so aggressive that they may swallow a lure.*

slower-moving sections of rivers, often concentrating near river mouths, where weed cover is heavy and the water is often turbid. In large lakes, they prefer heavily vegetated, muddy back bays and protected waters.

FISHING TACKLE Tackle for most pickerel fishing is lightweight. The grass pickerel is of negligible interest to anglers because of its small size, but the redfin pickerel does provide some sport in limited areas. Small spinners, spoons, and crankbaits are the rule for the redfin pickerel. A lightweight spinning outfit spooled with 4- to 6-pound-test line works best for most situations.

The chain pickerel provides considerably more sport than the redfin because of its larger size. Still, it's light tackle all the way for this scrappy and ferocious fish. Flashy silver spoons, spinners, and minnow-imitating crankbaits are a must for most lure selections. Because chain pickerel attack with such speed and voraciousness, they often totally engulf a lure, making it wise to use small, fine wire leaders to avoid breaking lines on the fish's teeth.

FISHING TECHNIQUES Techniques for catching pickerel are very similar to those used for catching the much larger northern pike. The

knowledge that pickerel often lie in ambush along weed edges makes fishing for them much easier. Most fish rest just inside the weed beds, facing out toward the open water, and will rarely move away from this cover to chase prey. The most productive method for catching these fish is to cast lures parallel to the weeds. Spinners, spoons, and crankbaits can be retrieved along weed lines, usually near the surface. If this doesn't produce any strikes, then the spinners and spoons should be allowed to sink closer to the bottom. They are then retrieved with the rod tip in the water to achieve a deeper depth for the lure.

The most productive technique for casting is to select short targets along the weed edge and then to move the boat along likely structures, making short overlapping casts all the while. The weed edges should be thoroughly covered in order to stimulate unaggressive fish into striking.

A PICKEREL, FOOLED BY A FLASHY SPOON.

S P E C I A L   T I P

Some of the largest chain pickerel come from backwater sloughs in lakes and in areas off the main slack water bays in rivers. These very shallow areas have an abundance of food, making the pickerel grow much faster. Also, because there is little current, pickerel spend less energy in their quest for food. Try weedless spoons in these areas in order to avoid getting hung up on the weeds. These spoons may also be used with a piece of pork rind or a twister tail to make them irresistible to hidden fish. You may catch a lunker!

Pike

COMMON NAMES great northern pick-erel, great northern pike, jack, jack-fish, northern pike, pickerel, pike, snake

DESCRIPTION This ferocious-looking fish is often referred to as the "water wolf," and the many tall tales about the pike are usually associated with its great size and distinctly predatory appearance. Pike are easily recognized by their characteristic sleek and elongated shape. The dorsal fin is positioned unusually close to the tail, and the fearsome head is dominated by odd duckbill jaws, filled with an abundance of large, sharp teeth. The northern pike's carnivorous appearance is reinforced by its malevolent stare and the green and yellow camouflage patterns that cover its muscular body. This fierce creature, once called the "pitiless pike," is a formidable sight indeed.

SIZE The North American angling record for pike was set by a leviathan that weighed in at 46 pounds, 2 ounces. This enormous pike measured more than 4 feet in length and was caught in New York's Scanandaga Reservoir in September, 1940. The largest Canadian pike reported was taken in 1890 from Lake Tschotogama in Quebec. It weighed in at an almost

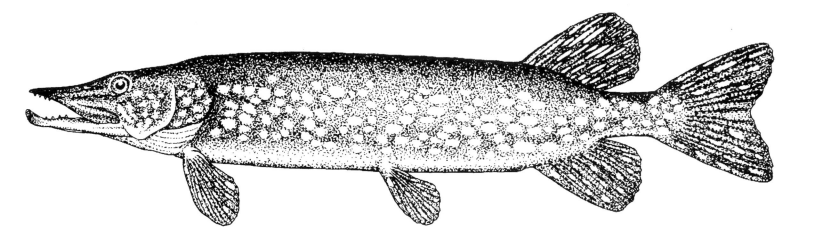

unbelievable 49 pounds. However, most fishermen are more accustomed to 18- to 22-inch pike, weighing an average of perhaps 3 pounds. Nevertheless, there may be monsters of 40 or more pounds lurking out there in Canadian waters – somewhere.

DISTRIBUTION The resourceful northern pike is a resident of the northern hemisphere. This extremely successful creature is one of the few species that is found throughout Canada. It is also found in many of the more northerly American states, especially Alaska. Although the pike prefers fresh water, this highly adaptable fish has even managed to occasionally extend its range into waters containing a low salt content.

BEHAVIOR AND HABITAT Northern pike use relatively simple tactics to capture their food. A feeding pike will frequently lie in ambush and then utilize its lightning speed to successfully attack its approaching and unsuspecting victim. Pike usually favor other fish as their prey, but

have also been known to gobble up frogs, mice, ducklings, crayfish, and various insects. They will forage on trout, bluegills, bass, whitefish, walleye, and burbot, although their dietary staples seem to be yellow perch, suckers, and other soft-finned fish. Pike are well known for

S P E C I A L   T I P

Pike will snap at anything that will fit into their jaws, and even a few things that won't. Yet, sometimes pike will be "off the feed" and nothing will seem tempting enough. Presentation is the key in such a situation. For these finicky pike, the angler should experiment with the retrieval speed and action of his lures. An erratic, stop-and-start retrieve along the surface with a floating Rapala, for example, will often draw a strike from a moody pike.

their voraciousness and will often attack fish of their own size and even of their own species. Anglers have frequently reported finding dead pike with large fish literally jammed in their throats.

Temperature and the availability of food are probably the most important factors that determine the various pike habitats. Northern pike will migrate to their spawning areas in the early spring as soon as the ice disappears, and the water reaches a temperature of 39 degrees Fahrenheit. Spawning locations usually consist of shallow bays, coves, rivers, and creeks. During the summer, pike are often found in weedy, shallow waters of 4 to 6 feet in depth. Many anglers, however, believe that the larger pike will inhabit the deeper waters of 40 or more feet. In winter, pike continue to feed and are often taken through the ice by anglers fishing over weed beds in depths of 10 to 20 feet.

FISHING TACKLE A large array of lures has been used to catch these superb game fish. The angler, however, often depends on "old reliables" such as large plugs, colorful

spinnerbaits, and various kinds of spoons. These proven types of lures work especially well when the fish are active and are located just off the weeds, in open water. New types of lures are the soft plastic baits, such as the Mister Twister. These are used alone or are rigged with weedless spoons and fluttered through the weeds. Because of the pike's numerous teeth, all of these various lures should be used together with a wire leader. Many anglers, especially fly-fishermen, will fashion their own leaders from extremely thin wire or even from 30- to 40-pound-test monofilament line. The fly-angler will use heavy gear consisting of a 9 1/2 foot, 9-weight outfit, preferably with a detachable fighting butt. Surface poppers and large, colorful streamers are the fly-angler's usual lure selections.

FISHING TECHNIQUES Northern pike respond well to a wide variety of fishing methods including trolling, casting, ice-fishing, and live- as well as dead-bait fishing. Even fly-fishermen have discovered the pike's magnificent sporting qualities.

NO WONDER THEY CALL THIS FISH THE "WATER WOLF."

QUICK TIPS

1 Pike are known to hide in some of the weediest spots imaginable. To fish these spots you can use weedless spoons but these have the disadvantage of having poor hooking power, particularly when the pike's bony mouth is taken into account. In weedy areas, bass surface lures such as Heddon's Dying Flutters can be very effective without constantly picking up subsurface weeds.

2 Most seasoned pike anglers use black wire leaders. In a pinch you can make your own pike leaders simply by purchasing heavy monofilament line (17- to 30-pound test) and some snap swivels and barrel swivels. These have the advantage of being cheaper and you can make them any length.

3 Pike usually slash at the bait to kill it before turning it in their mouths and swallowing. One of the problems of bait-fishing for pike is knowing when the bait is firmly in the pike's mouth so the hook can be set. This is largely solved with "quick-strike rigs," which have two hooks, one on each end of the bait. This means the hook can be set immediately.

4 In the early spring, the use of dead baits can actually out-produce live bait. This is because many bait fish have died after a long, hard winter and the pike are scavenging on them.

5 If you intend to release a pike, never handle it around the eyes or the gills. The best thing is to take the hook out while the fish is still in the water and gently cradle the fish until it swims away. If you intend to keep the pike, respect its sharp teeth and use a gaff.

Trolling is usually conducted with heavy short rods along weed lines or other structures with medium· to shallow-running lures, such as the red and white Daredevil spoon or a large bucktail spinner.

Thick weed beds, patches of lily pads, rock piles, and tree stumps are frequently the targets for anglers casting shallow-running spinners, spoons, and plugs. Spinning or bait-fishing outfits in the 6- to 7-foot range are most often used.

The ice-fisherman finds no difficulty in catching pike. They are hooked regularly with baited tip-up rigs and will also readily attack spoons, jigs, and specialty lures, such as the jigging Rapala. Special jigging rod-and-reel combinations are a must when fishing through the ice.

Bait-fishing is an extremely popular method of taking pike. Live baits, such as a whole chub or sucker, are fished with or without a large float between the mid-water level and the bottom. Dead baits also can be used successfully with the same methods or by retrieving them slowly. In either case, the pike is usually allowed to *run* with the bait and to stop before the hook is finally and firmly set.

Fly-fishing for pike is becoming increasingly popular because these hard-fighting fish are so readily available even during the doldrums of summer.

WHEN PIKE REACH THIS SIZE, HEAVY BAIT-CASTING GEAR IS CALLED FOR!

Pink Salmon

IN WEST-COAST WATERS, PINKS BECOME MIXED WITH OTHER SALMON DURING THE FALL RUNS.

COMMON NAMES humpback, humpback salmon, humpie, pink, pink salmon

DESCRIPTION The pink salmon is undoubtedly one of the most underrated and least pursued of North American salmon. Pound for pound, they are considered to be one of the best fighting salmon in North America. Unfortunately, the "humpies" of the west coast are reserved primarily for commercial interests, and they have not become as popular as the coho and chinook salmons.

Adults in the Pacific have steel-blue to blue-green backs, white upper bellies, and silver sides spotted with a limited number of black dots. Colors become less brilliant, the "hump" and kype (jaw) more pronounced in fresh water. Like other salmon, the males fight over females. The kype is a specialized weapon, and the humped backs serve to deflect attacks from other males.

SIZE Pinks, along with sockeye salmon, are the smallest of the North American salmons. Most adults returning to rivers are between 2 and 7 pounds, and a humpie over 10 pounds is considered to be large. The average pink probably weighs about 4 to 5 pounds.

DISTRIBUTION All native stocks of pink salmon occur in the Pacific and Arctic oceans, the Bering and Okhotsk seas, and the Sea of Japan. Humpbacks spawn in rivers in North America, from the Sacramento River in California, north to Alaska, including the Aleutian

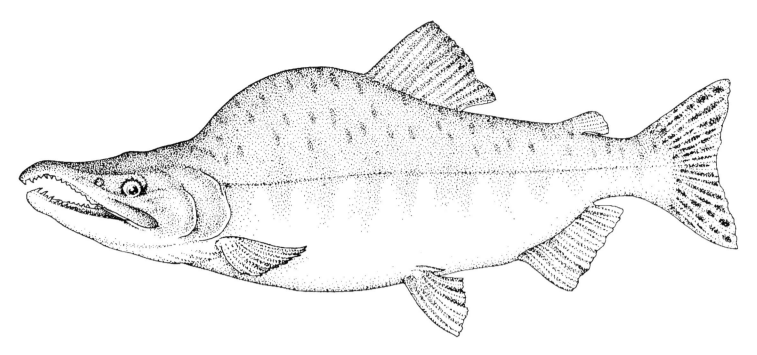

Islands, and east to the delta of the Mackenzie River. Stocks are most abundant in the central part of this range in the province of British Columbia. Abundance patterns also follow two-year cycles, with major spawning runs in southern British Columbia rivers, such as the Fraser, occurring in odd-numbered years, and major runs in northern rivers, in such places as the Queen Charlotte Islands, in even-numbered years.

Pinks were introduced in 1956 into Goose Creek, an Ontario tributary of Hudson Bay. This introduction failed, but fish from the same brood were released into Lake Superior, where they have since maintained a small population. Pink eggs from British Columbia were also planted into the North Harbour River in Newfoundland in 1958, and, by 1967, strays had spread to Nova Scotia, Labrador, and the Gulf of St. Lawrence in Quebec.

BEHAVIOR AND HABITAT Pink salmon remain in fresh water for only a short time after hatching, and many young do not feed at all until they reach the sea, where they feed on small plankton. Adults feed on similar small organisms, as well as fish and squid. Adults in streams feed little or not at all, but pinks in Lake Superior have been caught in rivers by anglers using live bait and small lures.

1 Roe bags are a good bait when the pinks enter the river. If the water is dirty from a heavy rain, the salmon will still hit if you make your offering more visible. This can be done by sliding a very bright plastic egg onto the line just above the hook's eye. Add an oversized, bright spawn sac and your "dirty water special" will be complete.

2 When a float is being used with spawn bags for pinks, always use a leader consisting of lighter line below the float. The light leader is usually tied on to a swivel, which also prevents line twist. If your bait snags up, the lighter line always breaks first, saving your float.

3 When the water is ultra-clear, single eggs are deadly for pinks, especially if there are spawning chinook or coho nearby. Single eggs that won't break up on the hook can be created by boiling loose salmon eggs until they become firm. Use them with light line, and the fish won't be able to resist.

4 By using ordinary food coloring you can tint trout or salmon eggs whatever shade you prefer, from gold to hot orange and pink. You can increase your odds for hooking hungry river pinks by throwing a handful of loose eggs into the pool before casting your roe bag or single egg.

5 When using small flies for pinks, try suspending them from a tiny float so that the fly just barely clears the bottom. Concentrate on brightly colored patterns and keep your eyes glued on the float, which will also serve as a strike indicator when a fish hits.

On the whole, pink salmon live two years. Adults return to spawning rivers after about eighteen months at sea. More than fifteen million pinks may return to major spawning rivers such as the Fraser, in odd-numbered years, from June through October. Exact timing depends on location. Many pinks spawn in tidal stretches of rivers or no more than 30 miles upstream, while others may ascend rivers for 300 miles or more before spawning. Pinks spawn on medium-size gravel, in redds up to a yard in length, and 1 1/2 feet deep. Hatching usually occurs from late December to late February, and young pinks soon migrate to tidal estuaries.

FISHING TACKLE For a long time pinks were "reserved" for commercial anglers and ignored by sport fishermen. Most pinks are caught incidentally by anglers targeting coho and chinook, so humpies often take the same lures as these other two salmons.

Since pinks are relatively small salmon, small baits and lures are most effective. The safest rule for

A sure-fire method for catching pinks is the jig-fly combination. Tie a small pink jig on your line, then tie a 4- to 6-inch leader on the line about 10 inches above the jig. At the end of this leader tie a small wet fly. Pinks that manage to turn down your jig presentation will be unable to resist the fly.

color is one of the simplest and truest in sport fishing: Pink for pinks. Other colors certainly catch humpies, but not with the same consistency as pink. Small pink spoons and hoochies are productive in salt and fresh water. Small spinners also catch this fish. A small tuft of pink yarn will produce dozens of pink salmon per day during peak runs in British Columbia streams and rivers. Pink or red is also the best for fly colors, though a touch of silver, and even black, is also effective.

FISHING TECHNIQUES River anglers usually find pinks mixed in with coho and chinook. Look for them in pools, in the slack water behind boulders, along rock walls, and in seams between slack and fast water. The freshest and most powerful fish are invariably found closest to the mouths of spawning rivers. Using a sensitive bait rod, cast yarn flies or a tuft of pink wool to fish in these areas, and you'll have continuous action. A No. 2 Laser Sharp or Gamakatsu is a good-size hook to use. Pinks readily devour fresh roe

that anglers use for coho and chinook – anglers fishing for these two game fish often cannot get their bait down through the ravenous schools of pinks.

One of the fastest-growing methods of fishing for pinks involves casting to milling schools in river mouths and estuaries. Anglers often wade out as far as they can, and using a 7- or 9-weight rod, cast a Polar Shrimp or similar fly tied to a sinking or sink-tip line. Pinks respond best to relatively fast retrieves achieved by line strips of about 18 inches. Do it right, and the action can be incredibly fast paced.

A GREAT LAKES PINK FALLS TO A ROE SAC.

Rainbow Trout

SCOTT RIPLEY

A RAINBOW
CRUISES THE
CLEAR WATERS
OF A STREAM
FOR FOOD.

COMMON NAMES bow, Kamloops trout, rainbow trout, steelhead, steelhead trout, steelie

DESCRIPTION The rainbow is among the top game fish in North America and in other parts of the world as well. True to its name, the rainbow often sports a variety of colors that vary with habitat, size, and sexual condition. Rainbows that live in streams and small inland lakes, and those that are closest to their spawning grounds, generally exhibit the darkest colors. Brighter, more silvery colors are the norm for lake residents. Stream trout also tend to be more spotted than the anadromous steelhead. To anglers, the definitive characteristics of rainbows, particularly the males, are their pink "cheeks" and the prominent pink-to-reddish stripe on their sides.

SIZE Rainbow trout vary considerably in size, depending mainly on their life history and the food base of their habitats. Resident trout in rivers tend to be smaller than most rainbows that feed in richer inland lakes. Most anglers across North America would probably agree that a 12-inch resident fish is a good catch from a river, though stream-dwelling rainbows do grow larger in Alberta's Bow River and in many of Alaska's larger rivers. Some of the largest inland-lake rainbows in

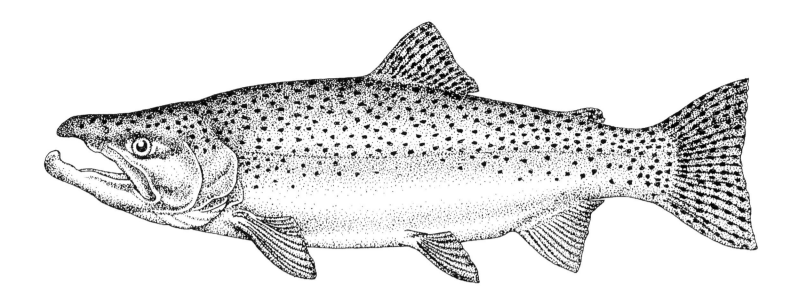

North America, however, are found in British Columbia. The famous Kamloops, as its name suggests, is found in the many lakes around Kamloops, B.C. Most do not exceed 5 to 7 pounds, but one taken many years ago in Jewel Lake, B.C. threatened to break the scales at 52 pounds.

DISTRIBUTION The native North American range of the rainbow trout is the eastern Pacific and much of the freshwater drainages of western North America. Due to extensive introductions, it can now safely be said to inhabit virtually all of North America where preferred habitat conditions can be met. Rainbows have also been introduced around the world, including New Zealand, Australia, Tasmania, South America, Africa, Japan, southern Asia, Europe, and Hawaii.

BEHAVIOR AND HABITAT Rainbows enjoy a varied diet, readily engulfing worms, small fish, all types of terrestrial and aquatic insects, fish eggs, and even the odd small bird or mammal. Most stream-dwelling

bows acquire most of their nutrition from insects and are therefore a perfect target for fly-fishers.

Resident stream rainbows inhabit riffles, pools, areas below waterfalls, undercut banks and brush, current breaks behind boulders, and other habitats that provide their

two essentials: food and cover. Lake rainbows enter streams to spawn in spring. Lakes without streams, however, rarely support sustainable populations of these trout.

FISHING TACKLE Gear for rainbows varies tremendously according to area, size of the fish, and angler preference. Rainbows are generally fished using one of three methods: bait, artificial lures, and flies.

Bait is a very popular choice of fishermen everywhere. Rainbows find worms almost irresistible, probably because they form part of a trout's natural diet. Trout can also be enticed with minnows and even a few less than natural baits such as corn kernels and cheese. Various eggs, grubs, and leeches will attract bows as well. Spinning rods that are fairly long and limber are ideal for bait-fishing. Small split shot pinched on the line can be used for weight, and small bait hooks are standard.

Rainbow trout are also drawn to spinners, plugs, and spoons, in a variety of sizes and colors. Mepps Aglia or Panther Martin spinners are especially effective. Spoons such as the E.G.B. or Pixie are very good also. Flatfish are a good lure for trolling presentations, and Rapalas are effective for rainbows in a wide range of conditions.

Rainbows readily take a wide variety of wet and dry flies. Much has been written about "matching

the hatch" when using these flies, especially in heavily fished areas where bows have been "educated" to recognize artificial flies. Basically, flies are either attractors that simply appeal to the trout's aggressive reflexes or imitators that mimic natural prey. Both types will work, providing the angler achieves a natural, drag-free drift and manages to put the fly in front of the fish. This is not always an easy task in deep lakes or in swift rivers.

Lake fly-fishing generally requires a full-sinking line, while river fly-anglers use floating or sink-tip lines. Fly rods are chosen according to the prevailing conditions and the size of the fish. Lighter rods (3-5 weight) are used for smaller stream fish and heavier rods (7-9 weight) are preferred for big fish in big rivers.

FISHING TECHNIQUES The best advice for anglers using any of these fishing techniques is to become familiar with the habits of the quarry. The angler should learn what constitutes good cover and feeding areas for stream trout. He should make a study of the insects that trout feed on in order to become a successful fly-fisher. In lakes he must know when the fish are deep, when they are shallow, and when they are likely to enter spawning rivers. In other words, knowledge of the ecology of the fish is more important than familiarity with the various types of trout tackle.

When the angler learns about the trout and their foods, he'll also know where and when they're most concentrated. Certain riffly sections of rivers are consistent producers, as are certain flats, bays, and river mouths of lakes.

THE RAPALA HAS TAKEN ITS SHARE OF RAINBOWS.

Rock Bass

ROCK BASS TAKE ON THE COLOR OF THEIR SUR-ROUNDINGS.

COMMON NAMES black perch, goggle eye, northern rock bass, redeye, red-eye bass, rock bass, rock sunfish

DESCRIPTION Yet another member of the sunfish family, this robust little fish is very appropriately named since it invariably chooses rock piles and boulders as its domain. The rock bass has a dark olive col-oration, mottled with darkish patches. However, when the rock bass moves to another background, its body color will quickly change in a chameleon-like fashion. The gill cover is tipped with black and the eyes are a reddish color, hence the name "redeye." The eyes also seem to bulge, which has led to the nick-name "goggle eye." This aggressive sunfish has a distinctly bass-like mouth, which, as many anglers will testify, is used to great advantage to attack almost anything that ven-tures near.

SIZE Rock bass are usually 6 to 8 inches long and weigh about the same number of ounces. Fish weighing over one pound are rarely caught by anglers. The record book does show two rock bass, however, that share the world title at 3 pounds. The first was caught in 1974, on the York River in Canada, the second in 1979, on Sugar Creek in Indiana.

DISTRIBUTION Rock bass are a very hardy fish. In the United States, they have spread from the St. Lawrence River southwards along the eastern flank of the Appa-lachian Mountains all the way to the Gulf coast in Florida, Missis-sippi, and Louisiana. In Canada, the rock bass flourishes in south-ern Quebec and in large portions

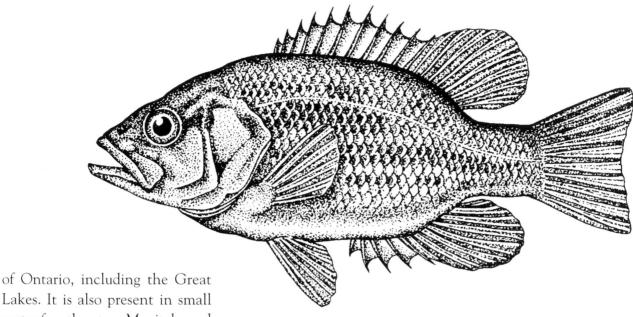

of Ontario, including the Great Lakes. It is also present in small parts of southeastern Manitoba and Saskatchewan.

BEHAVIOR AND HABITAT Rock bass favor small bodies of water such as cool, weedy lakes or streams, but are usually found near a rock bottom. In summer, adult rock bass will often school near deeper-water structures such as reefs, rocky points, or gravelly humps. These areas, in fact, usually harbor the larger fish. Rock bass will sometimes congregate in the same rocky areas as smallmouth bass and will also be found along weed lines, where they compete with many of the other sunfish species. In streams with rock bottoms, bass will avoid strong sunlight by dropping into deeper, obstructed pools or shady overhangs. This stream habitat seems to produce the very largest rock bass.

Rock bass are very aggressive feeders and will snap up terrestrial insects trapped on the surface film, various aquatic insects, crayfish, and other fish such as minnows, perch, and their own young.

Spawning occurs in northern waters from May to late June at water temperatures of 65 to 70 degrees Fahrenheit. In the south, spawning is already in full swing by

1 By far the best type of lure for rock bass is a crayfish-imitating lure, whether it be a jig or a crank bait.

2 Rock bass are quite tasty and provide a nice meal if you decide to keep a few for the frying pan. They can be gutted and cooked whole. They have very few bones to worry about.

3 Prime lakes for big rock-bass populations are lakes where there is an abundance of large game fish but no smaller ones. In this situation, the rock bass tend to take over as top-of-the-line predators in shallow water.

4 Often rock bass will be mixed in with other sunfishes that will take your lure more quickly. To get at the "rock-ies," it's often necessary to use a larger lure. If you are using live bait, then weight it more so that it drops to the bottom quicker. This will often put it closer to the rock bass.

5 Although most anglers think of periodically checking their knots when fishing for larger game fish like bass, pike, and muskie, it is equally important to check your line for nicks and abrasion with smaller fish. Nobody likes to lose their favorite crayfish jig to a small fish that breaks it off.

A SELECTION
OF SPINNERS
FOR GOOD OLD
RED-EYES.

March and April in water temperatures of 55 to 60 degrees Fahrenheit. Circular nests up to 2 feet in diameter are built by the males and defended aggressively after the female drops her eggs. In streams, rock bass will spawn in small secondary currents, in undercut banks, or downstream from obstructions such as log jams or rapids. Spawning sites in lakes usually consist of sand or gravel bars or shorelines with shady areas near boulders or logs.

During the fall and winter, when water temperature drops below 45 degrees Fahrenheit, rock bass become extremely sluggish and feed very little.

FISHING TACKLE A good panfish rod and reel will be a perfect outfit for rock bass. The rod-and-reel combination should be a good, balanced match and should be suitable for use with very light lines, lures, and baits. "Rockies" will eagerly take small spinners such as the Size 0 Mepps Comet or the Size 2 Rooster Tail. Small plugs such as the jointed Rapala, the Teeny Wee Crawfish, or the Teeny-R are also effective. Jigs and jig-spinner combinations such as those used for crappie and sunfish

In most cases rock bass do not require flashy lures to stir their curiosity. A return to basic techniques will usually do the trick. A good ultralight rod and reel with a matching premium-quality light line and an assortment of 1/16- to 1/8-ounce jigs are a very effective combination. Tube jigs in particular, fished slowly across the bottom, will outproduce most other types of lures.

are very popular for rock bass as well. Bucktail jigs, Beetle Spins, Fuzz-E Grubs, and Ugly Bugs all work especially well for rock-dwelling, bottom-feeding fish. Rock bass can also be taken by the fly-fisherman with streamers, hair bugs, wet flies, and poppers. Only the ice fisherman is left out since the rock bass slumps into near dormancy during winter.

FISHING TECHNIQUES Rock bass, because of their aggressive nature, can be taken with a wide variety of baits and lures by still fishing, casting, trolling, or fly-fishing. Bait fishermen use light lines and hooks somewhat larger than those used for other sunfish. A wide variety of baits are used, such as strips of fish flesh, worms, minnows, leeches, hellgrammites, or various terrestrial insects such as crickets or grasshoppers. These baits are effective in lakes or streams, which are fished by wading or by drifting in small craft such as canoes. Baits are often suspended under floats or used as trailing "appetizers" on small jigs and spinners. Since rock bass have larger and tougher mouths than other sunfish, they will take lures much more readily. In streams they are particularly vulnerable to lures during spawning as they defend their nests by aggressively striking out at anything that approaches them. They will also be especially susceptible to lures immediately after spawning when they feed voraciously and during the heat of summer when they drop back into the deeper pools. Lake fishing for rock bass in summer is somewhat more difficult since these fish often form loose schools and move into deeper water. The trick is to find these schools. Smaller rock bass, however, can always be relied upon to sit along the rocky shorelines of lakes, ever ready to hit the fisherman's lure, regardless of the time of day.

Sauger

A SLOW TROLL WITH A LIVE BAIT-RIG AT DUSK IS A NATURAL FISH CATCHER.

COMMON NAMES gray pickerel, gray pike, gray pike perch, sand pickerel, sand pike, sand pike-perch, sauger

DESCRIPTION The sauger is very closely related and similar in appearance to the walleye. Despite their uncanny similarities there are several clearly distinguishable differences. The walleye sports a noticeable white tip on the lower lobe of the tail fin; the sauger does not. Conversely, the sauger possesses distinct dark spots on its two dorsal fins, whereas the walleye may or may not have blotches of a much lighter color. Distinguishing between the sauger and the walleye becomes really difficult only when hybrids are encountered. These sauger-walleye hybrids are called "saugeyes" and may mix the characteristics of both species.

SIZE Another clear difference between the sauger and the walleye is size. Sauger are much smaller fish, a fact reflected in the world-record specimen weighing 8 pounds, 12 ounces, which was caught in Lake Sakakawea, North Dakota. This was a monster fish for this species but it pales in comparison to the 25-pound world-record walleye. Most saugers caught by anglers, weigh about 1 to 3 pounds, although fish of 4 to 6 pounds are common in specific areas such as the huge reservoirs along the Missouri River.

DISTRIBUTION Like the walleye, the sauger is a freshwater denizen and only rarely ventures into brackish waters. Its numbers, particularly in Canada, are much more restricted than those of the walleye, and its range is limited to the southwestern portions of Quebec, almost all of Ontario, and the southern half of the prairie provinces. Its American range, too, is somewhat smaller than that of its larger relative. Sauger occur from the Great Lakes southwards to Louisiana and the Tennessee River in Alabama.

BEHAVIOR AND HABITAT Once again the sauger is similar to its close relative, the walleye. Sauger prefer large, turbid bodies of water. They thrive in large reservoirs formed by dams on large river systems such as the Mississippi, the Missouri, and

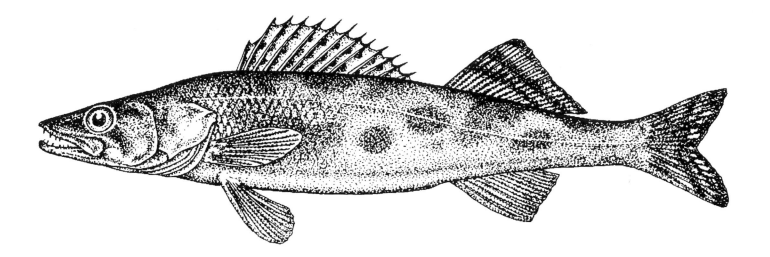

the Ohio, or in large lake systems such as the Great Lakes. The large reservoirs are ideal habitat for the sauger, which congregate near the dams and provide excellent angling. Efforts at stocking adult sauger in smaller bodies of water have consistently failed, and science cannot provide an explanation for this mystery.

Spawning occurs in spring, a short time after the walleye and often during the last weeks of May or first weeks of June. Shoals in lakes or river gravel are preferred, and the male sauger arrive at these spawning grounds before the females. During summer, sauger are found in the bays of large turbid lakes such as Lake Nipigon in Ontario. They adapt well to turbid or cloudy waters, possibly because the suspended particles of clay and other substances provide cover for their movements and also tend to concentrate forage for the fry near the water's surface.

Sauger are specialized night predators with a light-gathering membrane known as the *Tapetum lucidum*, which serves them especially well at night and in their turbid habitat. Their diet consists mainly of other fish such as shad, bass, freshwater drum, shiners, perch, walleye, burbot, chub, sticklebacks, and other sauger. In a pinch, sauger will also prey on leeches, crayfish, and even various insects.

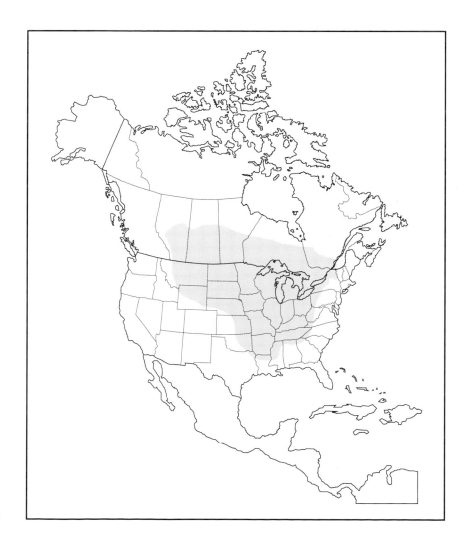

FISHING TACKLE Sauger have consistently turned up in anglers' catches in the larger Canadian lakes. In the United States they have actually become a major resource, especially during their seasonal runs in late fall and early winter in the tailwaters of large dams. Casting plugs, such as the small Thin Fin Silver Shad, the Fat Rap, or the Wiggle Wart, are often used, as are various smaller spoons and spinners. Perhaps the most popular artificial lures, however, are the huge array of jigs that have become available in tackle shops. These come in many sizes, styles, colors, and constructions and are especially effective in the deep, fast, and snag-filled waters near dams. Marabou and bucktail jigs are old favorites and have since been complemented by soft plastic creations such as the Mister Twister Sassy Shad, Twister Meeny, and Blue Fox Vibrotail. Other unique jigs have incorporated spinners, propellers, and spoons, such as the Whirly Bee, Cutie Pie, and Wigly Flipper.

FISHING TECHNIQUES Angling for sauger is, in most respects, similar to walleye fishing. Their flesh is exceptionally tasty, and although they are not known as superb

SPECIAL TIP

When trolling for sauger try a weight-forward Spinner-Live Bait rig such as the famous Erie Dearie or the Mepps Walleye Killer. These spiced-up lures will often induce slow-striking fish to become more enthusiastic. Indeed, even a simple piece of bright

yarn tied into the knot above the hook will greatly enhance a still-fishing or a drift-fishing presentation with live bait.

1 *Jig-fishing for sauger is highly productive, but on slow days it often takes some live bait tipped on your jig to ensure a good catch of fish.*

2 *Sauger love current and fast-water areas below dams. In these situations some extra split shot clamped onto your line ahead of your spinner, spoon, or crank bait will help it run deeper to get down to the fish.*

3 *In the turbid water that sauger prefer, try sticking to fluorescent colors to maintain the consistent action. Bright chartreuse, orange, and pink are top producers.*

4 *On really windy days, look for lake populations of sauger to move to shallow water in order to feed near shoals and rocky reefs where wave action will stir the water up and dissipate the sunlight.*

5 *When you use jigs for catching sauger, never exert a lot of pressure when playing the fish. Their teeth may be small, but they can still sever your line, and you don't want to lose that potential trophy.*

fighters they will readily take a lure or a bait throughout the season. Most sauger are routinely caught by walleye fishermen while bait-fishing, casting, trolling, or ice fishing and are often mistaken for small walleye. Live or dead minnows are used as bait in still fishing and ice-fishing for sauger. Like the walleye, sauger will mouth the bait very lightly, which means the angler must always be alert to slight movements. Other live baits include worms, leeches, and even the occasional crayfish. Ice fishermen frequently catch sauger with jigging lures sometimes tipped with a minnow. Trolling with appropriate plugs or spoons along weed lines, dropping ledges, or river mouths is also a highly effective technique. Because of the American sauger bonanza below reservoir dams, casting has become a prime method for taking sauger. Small spinners such as the Little Joe or Panther Martin, and spoons such as the Rok'T-Devlet or Little Cleo are effective, as are the various types of hard- and soft-bodied jigs. Regardless of the fishing style, the first challenge is to locate the fish and then to feel the extremely soft strikes on the bait or lure.

Smallmouth Bass

JIGS IN ALL THEIR
VARIETY ARE
PURE DYNAMITE
FOR SMALLIES!

COMMON NAMES black bass, brown bass, green bass, smallie, smallmouth, smallmouth bass, smallmouth black bass, white or mountain trout

DESCRIPTION The smallmouth bass has long been recognized as one of the feistiest of North American freshwater game fish. Indeed, when the angler first experiences a smallmouth fight he is invariably impressed by the vigorous leaps and frantic tailwalks. The smallmouth bass is shaped for ease of mobility and maneuverability under the

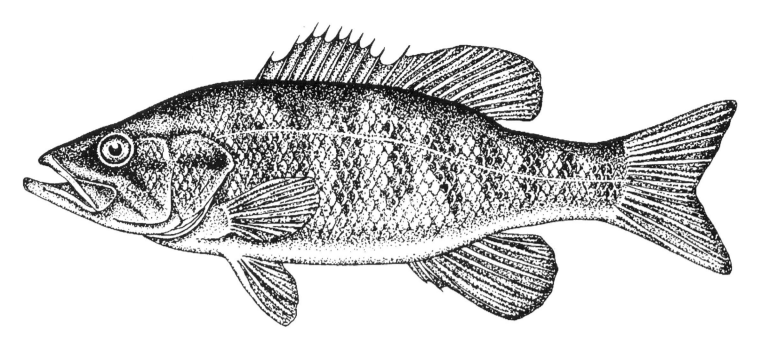

water and will use its attributes to dislodge the angler's hooks. Certainly stream smallmouth provide great sport, especially when hooked on light line. The smallmouth bass's coloring perfectly matches its environment. Weed-oriented smallmouth take on an obvious greenish hue, while those that are more often found near rocky lake shoals often exhibit varying shades of brown and light golden hues.

SIZE Although they are one of the most challenging of freshwater game fish, the average smallmouth bass weighs only 1 or 2 pounds. A 4-pounder is a real trophy, but a fair number of 5- to 7-pound fish are caught every year. The North American record stands at an intimidating 11 pounds, 15 ounces. It came from Dale Hollow Lake in Kentucky where quality habitat, optimum conditions, and a long growing season all contributed to produce this lunker. If you've experienced the fight of a 2-pound smallmouth, you'll be able to imagine the spectacular battle that this record fish must have mounted.

DISTRIBUTION Although the smallmouth bass was originally found only in eastern North America, it has now been introduced over a much wider area. It has been successfully stocked in most U.S. states and has had extensive success on Canada's east coast. Smallmouth

SPECIAL TIP

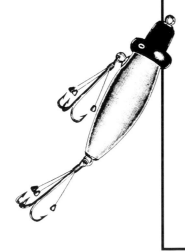

At times all anglers encounter fish that just seem to be off their feed. It's during these times that you have to pull a few tricks out of your pocket in order to tempt such "lock-jawed" fish into hitting your offering. One of the most popular techniques for these reluctant fish is "twitching." Stick baits, like the floating Rapala or Bomber Long A, are perfect for this tactic.

Simply cast out one of these lures, let it sit for a moment, twitch it so it swims erratically for a couple of feet, then let it sit. Repeat this maneuver as you reel your lure back to the boat. Notice that it looks like a helpless, injured minnow struggling near the surface — a perfect target for a hungry smallmouth. It's a dynamite technique when the fish seem to be asleep.

stockings in Nova Scotia and New Brunswick have thrived, and there are good populations in B.C., Saskatchewan, and Manitoba. The native populations in southern Ontario and Quebec have expanded northwards to Timmins in Ontario and Hull in Quebec.

BEHAVIOR AND HABITAT The physiology of the smallmouth bass dictates the kinds of prey it will eat compared to its bucket-mouthed relative, the largemouth. Typically, mature smallmouth will feed on a variety of aquatic insects, crayfish, and other fishes. Occasionally frogs will form a part of the smallmouth's diet, if they are available.

Throughout the early part of the season, lake populations of smallmouth are usually found in shallow to medium-deep water over rocky and sandy areas. The best holding areas have broken rock and rubble with lots of nooks and crannies, harboring an abundance of minnows and crayfish. If there is access to nearby deep water, the area will have even more potential for large numbers of smallies. When the water warms up considerably in mid-summer, most smallmouth move into water up to 30 to 40 feet in depth. These areas are often close to their early summer haunts because smallmouth are known to be "homebodies" who rarely move great distances throughout the year. In the fall, there is a general migration back to the shallow waters as the temperature drops. River smallmouth follow this same general pattern, feeding and holding in shallower water then retreating to deeper pools in the heat of summer.

FISHING TACKLE Fishing tackle for smallmouth bass is a relatively simple affair. Most anglers will opt for a medium- or medium/light-action spinning or bait-casting outfit designed to be used with 6- to 8-pound-test line. The often clear water habitat of the smallmouth dictates the use of light line to avoid spooking the fish. Because they are often caught in relatively open, snag-free water, the light-line technique is a productive yet reasonably safe approach.

One of the most popular lures for smallmouth is the jig. A marabou, a

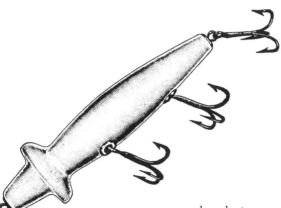

deer hair, or one of the popular series of Mister Twister plastic jigs, all are extremely productive for either lake or river smallmouth. Another popular type of lure is the crankbait. Minnow-imitating and crayfish-imitating crankbaits can be fished in shallow or in deep water and can be adapted for river use as well. Don't overlook small in-line spinners to tempt wary smallmouth.

The number-one live bait for smallmouth is undoubtedly the soft-shell crayfish, and these will usually out-produce all other baits. Running a close second and third are minnows and leeches, while hellgrammites are sometimes used in fast currents.

FISHING TECHNIQUES There are many popular techniques for catching

---

QUICK TIPS

1 *For really huge smallmouth, try a brown flipping jig with a brown or orange pork-rind trailer. This crayfish imitation is deadly for catching trophies, even under the toughest conditions.*

2 *To avoid having smallmouth jump and spit your hook, stick your rod tip into the water as you fight the fish. This helps keep the fish down,* *resulting in greater landing success.*

3 *Reeling in a crankbait along rocky shoals and sand bars and allowing it to actually bounce along the bottom will often trigger an onlooking smallmouth to hit. The noisy stirred-up bottom usually does the trick.*

4 *Windy weather usually attracts smallmouths. Fish* *the shallow sides of shoals, dropoffs, and other structures. Smallmouth bass will be drawn to these turbulent-water areas to feed on bait fish, crustaceans, and aquatic insects.*

5 *If you snap off the claws of crayfish, they will be less likely to crawl under rocks or grab onto weeds and spoil your presentation.*

smallmouth bass. These include casting a variety of lures, drifting with live bait, and even fly-casting on rivers and lakes. The versatility of casting lures makes this the most popular technique among anglers across North America. The sheer variety of effective presentations makes smallmouth fishing both enjoyable and rewarding. The jig is, perhaps, the most popular lure, especially when it is cast to rock piles and shoals and then slowly "hopped" along the bottom back to the angler. Minnow and crayfish colored jigs are tops for productivity. The Mister Twister Sassy Shad in the natural minnow color is one of the best jigs for most fishing situations. Crankbaits are sure to rank second in productivity. An effective technique consists of simply retrieving minnow-imitating lures adjacent to rock piles and along riprap. When using crayfish-imitating crankbaits, it's best to allow them to bounce along the bottom so they mimic the natural movements of smallmouth prey. Adding a couple of split shot a foot or so in front of your lure will help it reach bottom in deep water.

Bait-fishing for smallmouth in rivers involves casting their favorite food, the crayfish, into pools and current breaks. A lightly weighted bait will move naturally with the current so that the fish are not spooked. Bait-fishing in lakes is a relaxing sport. Many anglers simply drift over deeper structures, sand bars, and rocky breaks until they encounter a concentration of fish. They need only anchor in the area and enjoy nonstop action.

CRAWFISH CRANKBAITS ARE FIRST-CLASS SMALLMOUTH LURES.

Sockeye Salmon

A BIONIC BAIT JIG
COMBO FOOLED
THIS SOCKEYE.

COMMON NAMES: red salmon, silver salmon, sockeye, sockeye salmon

DESCRIPTION "Sockeye" is said to be a corruption of the Coast Salish Native Indian name "suk-kegh." Whatever the origin of its name, few other North American salmon are as famous as the sockeye for their spectacular migrations. Millions of crimson and green sockeye draw thousands of tourists to such renowned spawning sites as British Columbia's Adams River. Sockeye in this location are so thick that spectators often remark about walking across the river on the backs of the fish.

Sockeye are also famous among west-coast anglers as the best-tasting of all Pacific salmon. Their bright red flesh, which has a high oil and protein content, is highly sought after by sport anglers and commercial interests. Huge sockeye canneries once dotted the coasts of Alaska and British Columbia, testaments to the popularity of this salmon.

Ocean-going sockeye, and those in such freshwater hot-spots as Lake Washington, Seattle, are generally steel-blue to green-blue in color. They begin to darken soon after entering spawning rivers. The backs and sides of breeding males turn bright red to dirty red-gray. The area from their heads to their lower jaws is bright green to olive with black on the maxillary and snout; the lower jaw is white to gray. The dorsal, adipose, and anal fins are red, and the pelvic, pectoral, and caudal fins green to almost black. Females exhibit similar fin coloration, but the body is a darker, gray-red.

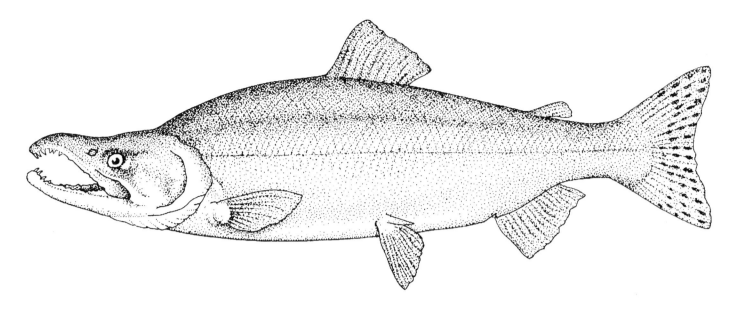

SIZE Sockeye are among the smallest of the Pacific salmon. The world-record sockeye from Alaska weighed just over 16 pounds, but the vast majority of fish caught by anglers range from 4 to 10 pounds. Nevertheless, ocean-going sockeye are much larger than landlocked sockeye, known as kokanee. Kokanee, which generally live up to four years of age, average 6 to 11 inches in length in British Columbia's Kootenay Lake, though fish over 20 inches and 4 pounds are occasionally caught.

DISTRIBUTION In North America, the sockeye ranges from the Klamath River in California north to Point Hope, Alaska. A spawning population inhabits Lake Washington in the busy metropolis of Seattle, and other runs of kokanee are found in many lakes throughout western North America. In Asia, sockeye are found from northern Hokkaido, Japan, to the Anadyr River in the Soviet Union.

BEHAVIOR AND HABITAT Ocean-going populations of sockeye feed mainly on shrimp-like plankton, but will also eat various bottom-dwelling organisms.

Sockeye move from offshore feeding areas to the mouths of spawning rivers from spring through fall. The timing of their arrival at river mouths depends on the time

of spawning and the distance to the spawning areas. From July through September, sport fishermen seek out concentrations of sockeye in the brackish water near the mouths of the Fraser, Somass, and other major spawning rivers in British Columbia. Sockeye runs usually reach peaks every four to five years. In 1990, some 20 million sockeye were estimated to have returned to the Fraser River. Usually at four to five years of age, sockeye move up these rivers from July through October. Sockeye generally spawn in rivers and streams that flow from lakes. They pass through the lakes to spawn in tributary streams. Eggs hatch in the spring, and the young sockeye spend from one to three

QUICK TIPS

1 *The most productive time of the year to fish for sockeye salmon is when they are scattered in the rivers just prior to schooling up for spawning.*

2 *Sockeye don't feed once they have entered rivers to spawn but anglers can fool them. Fish imprint on the prey they fed on as fingerlings in the river. A well-presented fly that imitates the forage of their youth can often trigger them into striking.*

3 *Because sockeye are soft hitters, you must have "sticky" sharp hooks for proper penetration.*

4 *Because sockeye feed on a variety of small invertebrates, you will have consistent catches if you use only small lures, such as spinners, spoons, and crankbaits.*

5 *Sockeye can be so spunky that you should use a tailing glove to more easily handle the fish.*

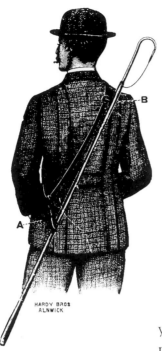

HARDY BROS
ALNWICK

years in the nursery lakes before migrating to sea.

FISHING TACKLE Serious sportfishing for sockeye is less than a decade old. This means that much of the tackle used to catch this salmon is of recent origin. It's hard to go wrong, though, if you remember two words: "pink" and "small." Most British Columbia anglers use pink hoochies – squid or plankton imitators measuring about 2 3/4 inches in length. Familiar pink hoochies include Nikka's MP-16, the Soco, and the Ross Bug-Eye Fly. All hoochies are tied with a short leader (24 to 30 inches) onto a small flasher such as the silver and pink Hot Spot, or the newly marketed Gibbs-Nortac Sockeye Flasher.

Anglers in Lake Washington have had success with a wider variety of tackle, including the U-20 Flatfish, PT Defiance spoons, and such plugs as the Hot Shot, Tadpolly, and Wiggle Wart. Some anglers have even had success trailing brightly colored, bare hooks behind dodgers. Best colors are reported to be pink, fluorescent red, nickel, and gold.

A variety of pink tackle, fresh baits such as roe, and even spinners and spoons will catch sockeye in rivers. Fishing for sockeye in rivers is not yet a major sport fishery in Canada because of federal Department of Fisheries closures, so tackle refinements are still to come. Flyfishers are probably ahead of other anglers when it comes to catching sockeye in rivers. Nymph patterns in pink, hot-green, flame, orange, ginger, and black all produce well.

FISHING TECHNIQUES West-coast anglers who consistently catch sockeye use what is known as the "Four-S" rule: sockeye, slow, straight, and small. Thus, they troll the small pink hoochies as slow and as straight as possible. Anchovies also catch sockeye, but not as many anglers use them as hoochies. Many anglers add another "S" to the formula: sparse. Some sockeye veterans trim down the "skirts" of their hoochies to make them sparser and more attractive to sockeye. The only exception to the small rule is hook size, as most hoochies are fitted with a large hook, usually a 3/0 or 4/0.

Trolling is done with downriggers

SPECIAL TIP

Sockeye are renowned as unparalleled table fare, but, among the salmon, their small size means that they can't match the fighting qualities of the larger salmon. This is true especially when the fight is hindered by the weight and drag of a flasher. Many west-coast anglers seeking to enhance the battle now use the Super

Release Dodger designed by Victoria charter skipper Wayne Laughren. The angler's line

pops free of the dodger as soon as a fish strikes, giving a drag-free and much-improved fight.

and slip weights, again using a flasher about 2 feet in front of the hoochie. Sockeye can be taken very close to the surface, but, at other times, they're concentrated at 60 to 70 feet, or deeper. Fish finders are a definite aid in finding concentrations of sockeye. Many anglers consistently troll with four rods, and double, triple, and even quadruple headers are not unheard of.

Perhaps the most exciting sporting aspect of sockeye fishing is attracting them to artificial flies. Some saltwater anglers have had success with flies, but fly-fishing for sockeye is mainly restricted to fresh water, and many fly-fishers claim that, pound for pound, sockeye fight better than steelhead. Sockeye are very soft takers, and they will not chase a fly farther than a few inches. Flies must be dead-drifted to them, and sockeye seem to take best where there is just enough current to keep the fly line swinging slowly.

Steelhead

(*see also* Rainbow Trout)

THERE'S
NOTHING LIKE
CATCHING A
STEELHEAD ON
A FLY.

COMMON NAMES bow, rainbow, steelhead, steelhead trout, steelie

DESCRIPTION The steelhead is simply the anadromous version of the rainbow trout. Although textbook definitions of "anadromous" refer to fish that spawn in freshwater rivers and then move to sea, most fisheries experts and anglers accept steelhead transplanted from the west coast into the Great Lakes as "steelhead" also. These fish simply use the Great Lakes as their "sea"

and run the tributaries to spawn.

Steelhead are characteristically a bright chrome/silver in color with little or no pink stripe running along their flanks when they are at sea or cruising the Great Lakes. However, when spawning time comes, they sometimes undergo a dramatic color change, become dark silver/olive with more pronounced spots. Their cheeks will become orange or reddish and the once-faint stripe along their sides now turns bright pink or even reddish in color. Steelhead also have numbers of black spots on their upper sides and back as well as on their caudal and adipose fins.

SIZE Steelhead usually grow to a much greater size than rainbows. Months of feeding in food-rich seas or lake waters can cause tremendous growth. The average steelhead caught in the Great Lakes watershed weighs 8 to 12 pounds, with some much larger specimens over 20 pounds recorded every year. Even bigger fish are common along the famous migratory rivers on the west coast of North America where

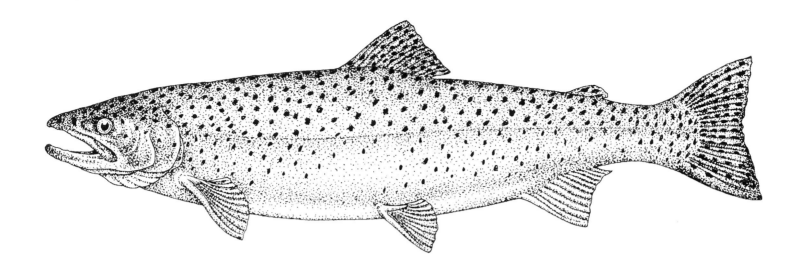

steelhead are often considered the supreme game fish.

DISTRIBUTION The native North American range of the steelhead is the eastern Pacific and much of the freshwater drainages of western North America. The most famous and successful introductions in North America of "true" steelhead from the west coast have occurred in the Great Lakes and their tributaries. These stockings have become enormously popular with anglers, and the fish have maintained vigorously reproducing populations.

BEHAVIOR AND HABITAT The diet of the steelhead varies with their habitat and location. Great Lakes fish feed heavily in the summer months on vast schools of alewife and smelt. Their saltwater brethren feed extensively on shrimp when young, then graduating to a variety of fishes. When steelhead move into streams and rivers to spawn, their feeding activity slows but does not stop altogether. They will engulf drifting eggs, small stream-dwelling fishes, and a variety of aquatic insects.

Great Lakes steelhead often roam the upper layers of the water, following the baitfish schools during the summer months. Locate the baitfish and you will also locate the "steelies." Of particular interest to anglers is the behavior of the steelhead once it enters the streams and

rivers on its way to the spawning grounds. In the stream environment, it behaves just like the native stream-dwelling rainbow. It relates to riffles, pools, waterfalls, undercut banks and brush, boulders, and other habitats that provide current breaks or cover.

FISHING TACKLE Gear for steelhead is necessarily heavier than for native rainbows. Migratory fish are quite a bit bigger in size and therefore require longer rods with much more backbone. West-coast and Great Lakes steelheaders often use special float-fishing, bottom-bouncing, or fly-fishing gear. Bait anglers use a variety of fresh, prepared, or imitation roe in the single-egg or roe-bag form, depending on the conditions at hand. Big-river anglers will often fish out of drift boats, trolling a variety of wobbling plugs or spoons. Yarn flies and other roe imitations are also drift-fished from boats.

Great Lakes fishermen, seeking their quarry on the "big water" during the summer, will employ planer boards and downriggers to present a variety of spoons or wobbling plugs to cruising pods of steelhead.

FISHING TECHNIQUES One of the most important factors in successful steelheading is knowing when the fish are moving into their spawning rivers and recognizing prime conditions for catching a mess of trout. Usually the most critical factors to

Nymph patterns are often very effective trout flies for rivers, but takes can be light, so a strike indicator is needed. Don't pass up a chance to tempt steelhead with a black marabou pattern, which has a highly visible silhouette and

seductive action. Hot pink is another good bet for steelhead. In B.C., one of the best baits for steelhead, especially for fish that have been in the river for a while, is undoubtedly the sand or ghost shrimp. This bait consistently outproduces roe and artificials on many rivers.

If you're still having trouble tempting those steelies because of heavy angling pressure, consider fishing at night. Many tackle shops sell "glow in the dark" beads. Add some bait, "charge" the bead with a flashlight or photo flash, and fish the trout at night when they feel most secure – without a crowd.

success are temperature and precipitation. Heavy spring rains cause rivers to swell, bringing in many fresh, aggressive fish. Most anglers develop a feel for when the fish will start biting. Rain brings in the fish but usually they won't hit when the rivers are too high and roily. When the rivers start to clear, the fishing peaks. A good knowledge of the rivers and streams in your area will enable you to pick and choose the best spots. Some rivers clear up quickly, while others may take several days after a big storm.

The timing of steelhead runs are more or less consistent from year to year, with some variations resulting from water levels. Many steelheaders fish the peaks of runs in various rivers, moving around to hit the strongest runs. In some rivers, such as Michigan's Au Sable, the trout feed most consistently at night.

And don't forget that anglers can successfully fish for steelhead through the ice. Diehard winter steelheaders will fish frozen river mouths with Swedish Pimples and Jigging Rapalas.

STEELHEAD LITERALLY CROWD INTO THEIR NATIVE STREAMS.

Striped Bass

THE NOVICE STRIPED BASS ENTHUSIAST OFTEN HIRES THE SERVICES OF A CHARTER BOAT.

COMMON NAMES rockfish, striped bass, striper, striper bass

DESCRIPTION The striped bass has long been recognized along the eastern coast of North America as a commercial as well as a sport fish. Its introduction to the west coast, back in the late 1800s, has provided a phenomenal sport fishery there as well. This originally anadromous species has even made the transition to landlocked lakes and impoundments, which have been created from the erection of dams along coastal watersheds.

The striped bass is much bigger than the smallmouth, largemouth, and spotted bass. Its colors include a dark olive green to black on the back, fading to silver on the sides, and then to white on the belly. The five to eight stripes, running horizontally along the sides of the fish, have given the striped bass its name.

SIZE The striped bass can weigh more than 50 pounds in landlocked lakes. Saltwater anglers have caught specimens weighing more than 75 pounds. There have even been reports of striped bass breaking the 100-pound mark. The average Canadian fish, caught by anglers on the east coast, is usually between 3 and 4 pounds. Along the more southerly coasts of the United States, fish averaging between 10 and 20 pounds are common. The striped bass is a schooling fish, and often vast schools will feed on the surface, enabling anglers to quickly catch their limit.

The current IGFA all-tackle record for landlocked striped bass is a California fish of 66 pounds. The world-record sea-run striper stands at 78 1/2 pounds. This magnificent specimen was caught in Atlantic City, New Jersey.

DISTRIBUTION The striped bass is primarily a coastal fish native to Atlantic waters from the St. Lawrence River in Quebec down to northern Florida, occasionally in the Gulf of Mexico from Florida to Louisiana, and also along western coastal waters from Washington down to California. Concentrations of these fish occur in the San

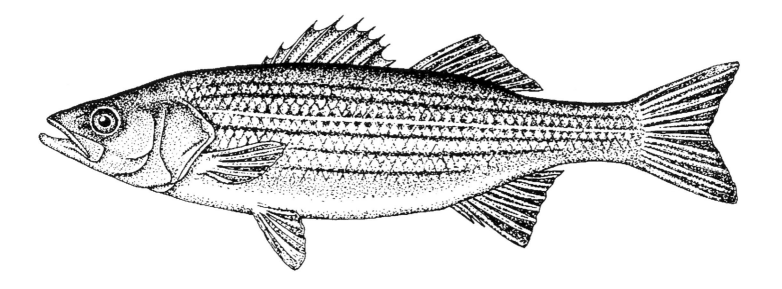

Francisco Bay area in the west and from Massachusetts down to North Carolina in the east. Healthy landlocked populations of striped bass occur in impoundments in the southeastern states and, more recently, in California.

BEHAVIOR AND HABITAT Striped bass are voracious feeders, often roaming in massive schools. It's truly an awe-inspiring experience to encounter them feeding on the surface in the spring and fall. The feeding is often short but very intense as the fish first gorge themselves and then abruptly dive into deeper water. Landlocked striped bass feed heavily on shad in many freshwater impoundments, although other forage fish such as smelt, alewives, and menhaden also make up a significant part of their diet when available.

Sea-run striped bass spawn in rivers, and the landlocked fish will do this as well if there are medium to large river systems draining into their impoundments. Spawning takes place in the spring, making stripers easily accessible to anglers. After spawning, these fish will roam coastal waters, feeding in quick spurts.

Landlocked stripers move into fairly deep water in the summer and will feed in spurts. It seems that during a feeding rampage, all striped bass begin and stop feeding at the same time. Freshwater stripers are often found schooling in deep water

Striped bass are known to be moody feeders. They will feed for a very short time before completely shutting down their activity. The best way to tip the odds in your favor is to concentrate your angling efforts during known peak feeding times and to relax during inactive periods. The best times to fish for freshwater stripers occur during low-light conditions. Early morning, late evening, and night are all prime times. For some great striper action in coastal waters, fish the two hours before and after a tide change, especially when this coincides with low-light conditions.

SCOTT RIPLEY

during the summer, except for some rises to the surface during a feeding frenzy. The most important factor governing their location is the movement of the bait fish that they prey upon. If these bait fish are found, the striped bass will usually not be far off.

FISHING TACKLE Tackle for striped-bass fishing is varied but definitely leans toward the heavyweight side. Ordinary freshwater fishing usually only requires medium-weight spinning or bait-casting outfits spooled with 10- to 14-pound-test line. However, saltwater or deep-water fishing in impoundments requires heavyweight outfits spooled with up to 30-pound-test line.

Freshwater or saltwater surface-feeding fish can be taken with a variety of topwater chugger- and popper-type lures. When striped bass are not feeding on the surface, the best lures for casting are spoons, jigs, and crankbaits in both salt and fresh water. Saltwater anglers will also add imitation squids to their arsenal.

FISHING TECHNIQUES Striped bass can be taken using angling methods such as casting, trolling, drift-fishing, and even fly-fishing. Live bait and lures hold equal weight among anglers as the preferred way to "sucker" a striper.

The most exciting way to catch striped bass occurs when they are schooling on the surface. Anglers will roam near known schooling hot-spots, looking for signs of feeding activity. Circling gulls and terns will often signal an area where feeding stripers have pushed a school of bait fish to the surface. When this occurs, anglers rush to the spot to cash in on feeding frenzies that are often all too brief. Usually two rods are rigged up, one with a topwater lure, the other with a spoon or crankbait in case the fish descend into deeper water.

Trolling with baits or lures is also a popular technique in both fresh and salt water. Often bait will be hooked to a spoon or spinner and trolled over a variety of depths until fish are located.

Drifting and casting with live bait is also a productive technique for striped bass. The most widely used coastal live bait is the sea worm, although a variety of other baits are also used. Often the bait is suspended under a float in shallow coastal waters and tributaries. In fresh water, where the fish may be located in very deep water of over 40 feet, live bait such as gizzard shad are frequently drift-fished. The key to success, however, is to locate the fish, and often this requires the use of sonar to pinpoint their location.

A SELECTION OF GREAT, TOP WATER STRIPER LURES.

Sturgeon

LAKE STURGEON
ARE WELL CAM-
OUFLAGED WITH
A WHITE BELLY
THAT BLENDS IN
WELL WITH THE
SURFACE OF THE
WATER.

COMMON NAMES Lake sturgeon: bony sturgeon, common sturgeon, red sturgeon, rock sturgeon, ruddy sturgeon, shell-back sturgeon, smooth-back, stone sturgeon

White sturgeon: Columbia sturgeon, Oregon sturgeon, Pacific sturgeon, Sacramento sturgeon

DESCRIPTION Both of these sturgeons have a very primitive appearance that echoes their ancient origins, which can be traced back all the way to the Upper Cretacious era.

The torpedo-shaped lake sturgeon is partially covered with three rows of bony plates or shields. The cone-shaped snout has four barbels on either side. The toothless mouth is beneath the snout and is specialized for sucking food from the bottom. The fish's color is a basic brown with a white belly. Black blotches are present near the snout and along parts of the back.

The white sturgeon has a body that is more rounded than the lake sturgeon's, and the snout is broad and flat rather than pointed. There are also several rows of bony plates running along the body. The toothless mouth is designed for bottom feeding and there are two barbels on either side. This sturgeon's color ranges from a dull gray, olive or brown along the back to white on the belly.

SIZE Lake sturgeon grow very slowly. Males of the species can live for up to fifty-five years, while females are capable of reaching eighty years of age. Sexual maturity is not reached before the age of twenty. These sturgeon can, however, attain great size. Fish of over 100 pounds are common and sturgeon of almost 8 feet in length, weighing over 300 pounds have been caught.

White sturgeon are the largest freshwater fish in North America. Growth rates are very slow and sexual maturity takes between ten and twenty years. Fish weighing hundreds of pounds are caught each year, but even these are dwarfed by the giants that are occasionally taken. The world-record white sturgeon stands at 394 pounds, but much larger fish, some weighing over 1,800 pounds, have been reported.

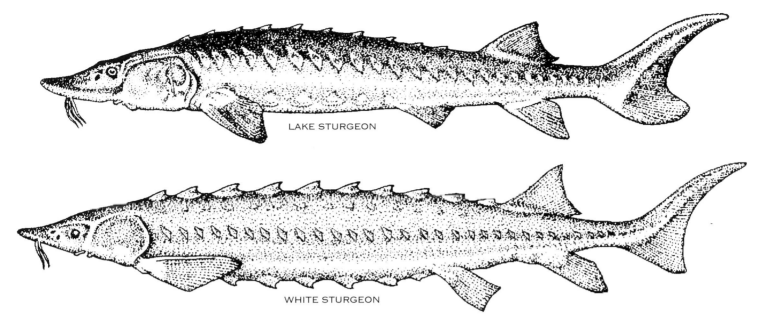

LAKE STURGEON

WHITE STURGEON

DISTRIBUTION Lake sturgeon have a wide distribution in lakes and rivers from the St. Lawrence River to Hudson Bay and all the way to the North Saskatchewan River in Alberta. In the south, this sturgeon's range includes the area from the Mississippi River to the Tennessee River in Alabama and Mississippi.

White sturgeon are restricted to the Pacific coastline from Alaska to California. In Canada they are found in the Fraser River, Taku River, Kootenay River, and the Columbia River.

BEHAVIOR AND HABITAT The lake sturgeon occurs in both rivers and streams and prefers fairly shallow waters. Spawning takes place in streams during the spring, some time between April and June, although there have been reports suggesting lake spawning as well. Sturgeon eggs are stuck to gravel on the bottom. Although the very young fish feed on planktonic organisms, a sturgeon of 6 or so inches in length is already capable of feeding on insect larvae, mollusks, crayfish, and plant material, all of which

are sucked into the specialized, tube-like mouth. Typical sturgeon feeding behavior consists of constantly moving about until interesting material is found and sucked into the mouth. All nonedible matter is quickly ejected, while the food is methodically worked until it can

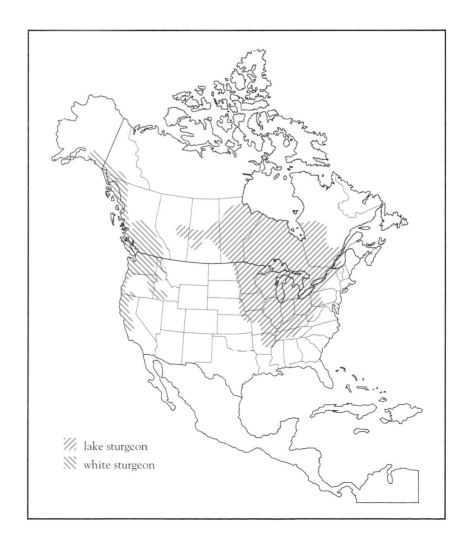

lake sturgeon

white sturgeon

SPECIAL TIP

Here's a tip for really big lake sturgeon. The fish can be located using a sonar unit around river mouths and lake shoals. Once located, a proven walleye technique can be used to catch them. The bait is weighted with an egg sinker and dropped to the bottom. In the meantime, the angler very slowly trolls back with the boat, gradually moving the bait around in the sturgeon's feeding grounds until the fish's keen senses enable it to locate and take the bait.

A CLOSE-UP OF A STURGEON'S HEAD, SHOWING THE BARRELS AND THE TOOTH-LESS MOUTH.

be swallowed. Feeding usually takes place in areas with a mud or a mud-gravel bottom. The lake sturgeon locates its food by means of its constant roving and the sensory ability of its barbels.

The white sturgeon often spends much of its life in the Pacific Ocean and only ascends the rivers and streams of the west coast to spawn. Spawning occurs between May and June, usually above a rocky bottom in fast currents found near waterfalls or rapids. Enormous numbers of eggs are released, (almost 700,000 for a 35-pound female), and adhere to the rocks on the bottom. The white sturgeon feeds on crustaceans, mollusks, insect larvae, and various other bottom-dwelling life. It uses its specialized mouth and sensory barbels to search out food on the bottom. Once this sturgeon surpasses a length of 19 or so inches, however, other fish become the dietary staple. Sculpins, sticklebacks,

other sturgeon, and lamprey eels have all been found in the stomachs of white sturgeons.

FISHING TACKLE "Sturdy" is the best word to describe sturgeon fishing tackle. Many anglers use Penn star drag reels and strong, stiff rods of about 5 or 6 feet in length. The idea is to employ tackle that will be able to handle fish that may weigh hundreds of pounds in fast currents. Lines should also be sturdy. For lake sturgeon, lines of between 20- and 30-pound test are used along with large, super-strong cadmium hooks. For white sturgeon, line strength is generally doubled to the 40- to 60-pound range and even larger cadmium hooks are employed.

FISHING TECHNIQUES Sturgeon fishing is invariably bait-fishing. Lake sturgeon are often caught by surprised anglers using setlines for other species such as catfish or carp. They are often taken from shoals in large rivers or lakes in 15 to 30 feet of water and have been caught using bait fish such as American shad.

White sturgeon are often sought by anglers who are impressed by their sheer size and strength. These anglers look for the fish in the fast current sections of rivers and use baits such as liver, cut minnows, worms, or whole eels. On the Fraser River in British Columbia, the top bait is the young of the parasitic lamprey eel. To get the bait down to the bottom, they use pyramid sinkers, ranging in weight from 8 ounces to 1 pound, depending on depth and current. These sinkers are suspended from a dropper line and the bait is between 12 inches and 3 feet from the junction between the dropper and the main line. Often large numbers of sturgeon will be held up by a dam or rapids and can readily be caught using this simple method. A sturgeon take is nothing more than a steady but determined pulling on the line after the fish has sucked up the bait.

A FINE WHITE STURGEON CAUGHT IN THE FAST CURRENTS OF A SPAWNING RIVER.

SCIENTIFIC NAMES Pumpkinseed: *Lepomis gibbosus*
Bluegill: *Lepomis macrochirus*
Green sunfish: *Lepomis cyanellus*
Redbreast sunfish: *Lepomis auritus*
Redear sunfish: *Lepomis microlophus*

Sunfish

YET ANOTHER
PUMPKINSEED
IS FOOLED
BY A WORM.

COMMON NAMES Pumpkinseed: common sunfish, pond perch, sun bass, yellow sunfish

Bluegill: blue sunfish, bream, copperbelly

Green sunfish: blue-spotted sunfish, green perch, rubbertail, sand bass

Redbreast sunfish: longear sunfish, redbreast bream, yellowbelly sunfish

Redear sunfish: shellcracker, stump-knocker, yellow bream

DESCRIPTION The various sunfishes belong to the family *Centrarchidae*. Surprisingly, the smallmouth and largemouth basses also are members of this diverse North American group. Sunfish are a very prolific and delightfully colored group of fish. Youngsters will often first learn the joy of fishing from these bold rascals who seldom hesitate before striking.

One of the most common sunfishes, the quaintly named pumpkinseed, is easily recognized by its olive-colored body and the conspicuous black center, yellow rim, and bright red spot on the "ear flap" extension of its gill cover.

The bluegill may vary greatly in color, ranging from yellow to dark blue or even seem transparent. It does, however, usually possess a black or bluish ear flap.

The green sunfish is usually olive green with a larger black blotch and red border on the ear flap and a larger mouth than the bluegill.

The redbreast sunfish proudly sports a dazzling blend of orange and red along its belly and possesses a distinctive elongated black tip on its gill cover.

The redear sunfish may closely resemble the pumpkinseed but its gill flap is flexible and will bend at right angles, unlike the gill cover of its look-alike relative.

SIZE The sunfish clan, with the exception of the various basses, is not known for producing leviathans. A pumpkinseed 8 inches long and weighing 1/2 pound is considered a good catch, and the species world record is only 12 1/2 ounces.

Bluegills seldom exceed 10 inches in length or 1 pound in weight,

PUMPKINSEED

BLUEGILL

although the world record is an astonishing 4 pounds, 12 ounces.

The green sunfish averages 5 or so inches in length and seldom exceeds a pound in weight, although two fish share the world record at 2 pounds, 2 ounces.

Adult redbreast sunfish average only about 4 ounces in weight, and the world record weighed in at an even 2 pounds. Most redears are only 7 to 10 inches long, but, once again, the world record is an amazing 4 pounds, 8 ounces.

DISTRIBUTION Pumpkinseeds occur coast to coast in the northern United States and the extreme south of most Canadian provinces, including all of Ontario.

The bluegill's range extends throughout most of the continental United States as well as some extremely southerly portions of Canada, most notably Ontario.

Green sunfish too are found in most American states and the southern portions of some Canadian provinces, especially Ontario.

Redbreasts are restricted to the American east coast, the northern Gulf states, and parts of New Brunswick in Canada.

The redear's range is limited to the southeastern United States and a few locations in the southwest.

BEHAVIOR AND HABITAT The pumpkinseed has been stocked in many

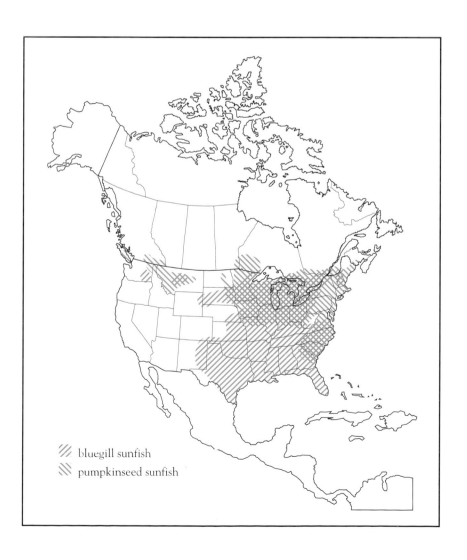

bluegill sunfish
pumpkinseed sunfish

QUICK TIPS

1 *Because the various sunfishes are readily available throughout most parts of North America, they are a great way to introduce the very young to the enjoyable sport of fishing. Don't keep them out too long on their first few outings, especially if the action is really good. They can easily get bored by the repetition of* catching so many fish.

2 *If you're live bait-fishing and run out of worms, simply look around for insects like beetles or grasshoppers. They make a great substitute for worms and keep the fish biting.*

3 *Don't use the hooks commonly sold in most stores for worm-fishing with a bobber. Often they are much too big for tiny bluegill or pumpkinseed mouths. The best hooks to use are small fly-tying hooks that have a long shank but a small hook gap. They are* easily removable from the fish's mouth and yet are the perfect size for the fish to engulf.

4 *Use one or two split shot to weigh down your live bait when fishing for panfish. Bell sinkers and other weights that are commonly used are simply too heavy and make feeling the fish bite much more difficult.*

5 *Try fly-fishing for panfish with a variety of attractor-pattern dry flies such as poppers and hoppers for honing your skills and having a lot of fun, too!*

BLUEGILL ARE
A PANFISH
FAVORITE.

American states and prefers slightly cooler waters with shallower depths and more vegetation than other sunfish. They can often be found in smaller, shallow lakes, sheltered bays, or slow-moving rivers. Pumpkinseeds feed mostly on insects but will also take the odd snail or small fish.

Bluegills prefer clear, calm, or slow-moving water with medium weed growth, although they will adapt to turbid and even slightly brackish water. They will feed opportunistically on insects, crustaceans, other fish and even aquatic plants.

Green sunfish are the "tough guys on the block" and are able to tolerate conditions of low oxygen, changing temperatures, and murky water, although they prefer areas with heavy cover and only moderate current. Green sunfish with their large mouths are able to prey regularly on other fish.

Redbreast sunfish, too, are highly adaptable and are at home in fast or still water, in lakes or in rivers. They prefer the deeper, weedy areas of rivers or lakes with a sand or mud bottom. Redbreasts feed on aquatic insects, crustaceans, and various small fish.

The redear prefers clear water with only moderate weed cover and will haunt stumps, boulders, or other shady structures, often in deeper water. Redears will feed eagerly on insect larvae, but are often called "shell-crackers" because of their propensity for feeding on snails.

FISHING TACKLE The various sunfish are renowned more for their

constant willingness to take lure, bait, or fly rather than for their fighting abilities. To be fair, sunfish try to give a good account of themselves when hooked, but their diminutive size often works against them. For the sporting angler, the type of fishing rod and reel thus becomes important. Ultra-light rods and reels, combined with very light line in the 2- to 4-pound-test range, will give the angler added sensitivity, which will add to the enjoyment of the "heat of battle." Such ultra-light equipment also gives the angler an outright advantage when working with the extremely small and light lures that are used for sunfish. The variety of sunfish lures is endless. Small spinners such as the Size 0 Black Fury or the Size 2 Rooster Tail are "can't miss" lures. Just about any very small spoon, such as the Daredevil or the Mepps Spoon, will take sunfish. Similarly, tiny plugs, such as the Thin Fin XT, Sonic, or Teeny-R, will produce panfish. In faster currents or deeper water, jigs or jig-spinner combinations, such as the Fuzz-E-Grub or the Beetle Spin, will work wonders.

Sunfish are particularly suited for the fly-fisherman. Fly rods of 7 to 8 feet in length are used with No. 5. or 6 fly lines. Since sunfish are anything but shy feeders, many fly-anglers use surface lures with floating lines. Hair bugs such as the Black Gnat, Rubber Spider, or Wooly Worm are favorites, along with the various lightweight poppers.

FISHING TECHNIQUES Since the sunfish clan is constantly on the alert for a snack, the angler can enjoy good fishing using almost every method known to the sport. Although not known for their ferocity, sunfish will usually pursue anything that doesn't actually frighten them. They will snap up almost any natural bait, including worms, grasshoppers, mayfly nymphs, crickets, leeches, meal worms, and minnows. Care should be taken to use *small* baits with light hooks, lines, and sensitive bobbers. Lures, too, should always be very small and light and will often outproduce live baits. This is especially true when the sunfish are belligerently guarding their nests.

Walleye

BIG WALLEYE
LOVE STRUCTURE
LIKE THIS MAN-
MADE BREAK-
WALL.

COMMON NAME pickerel, pike-perch, walleye, wall-eyed pickerel, walleye pike, wall-eyed pike-perch, yellow walleye

DESCRIPTION Probably one of the most popular game fish in North America, the walleye is best known for its large, glassy eyes and its nocturnal habits. In spite of their potential for large size, walleye are members of the innocuous perch family. "Old mooneye," as the walleye is sometimes known, can be detected at night by shining a flashlight on the water. The fish's specialized eyes contain an extremely light-sensitive layer that is highly reflective and glows eerily under the light. In daylight, the walleye is easily recognized by the white tip on the lower lobe of the tail. The walleye has a well-camouflaged and fierce appearance. This fish is a very successful predator, with numerous prominent and obviously business-like teeth. Although walleye populations have been very successful, especially as a result of extensive stocking programs, another subspecies, the blue pike or blue walleye, was decimated by a combination of overfishing and habitat changes and is now listed as extinct.

SIZE The world-record walleye was caught in Old Hickory Lake in Tennessee and weighed in at a whopping 25 pounds. Although individuals in northern walleye populations will grow much more slowly than their southern counterparts,

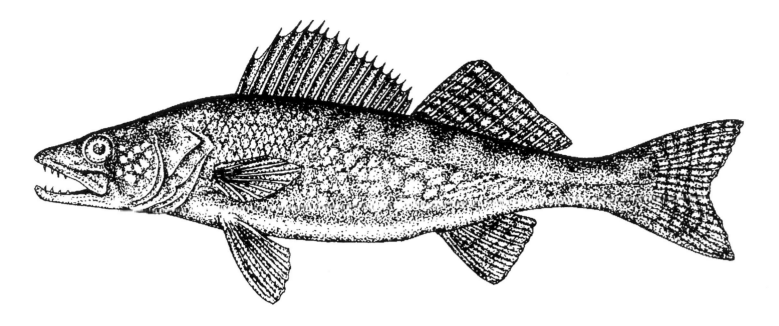

huge walleye are regularly taken in Canada, especially in areas such as the Bay of Quinte and the Moon River in Ontario. The average walleye caught by anglers weighs about 1 1/2 to 2 pounds but monsters of 10 to 12 pounds are common, especially in Ontario where a long-term stocking program has been paying spectacular dividends.

DISTRIBUTION The walleye is a freshwater resident that will only rarely wander into brackish waters. As such, it is a very successful species and ranges from Quebec throughout much of the eastern United States, all the way to the Gulf coast in Alabama. Although the walleye does not flourish in Labrador and the Atlantic provinces, its range includes large areas of Quebec, Ontario, and the prairie provinces and even a tiny northeasterly portion of British Columbia and the Northwest Territories. The walleye has even established a strong presence in the Northwest Territories in a broad belt following the Mackenzie River, Great Bear Lake, and Great Slave Lake.

BEHAVIOR AND HABITAT Walleye mature at two to four years of age for males and three to six years of age for females, and are able to thrive in a wide variety of environments. Their ideal habitat, however, is a large, shallow lake with cloudy water conditions suitable for the walleye's

extremely light-sensitive vision. In clear water, walleye will feed almost exclusively during low-light times, such as late evening or night.

Walleye are also found in large streams and rivers that contain deep or turbid water, which screens out some of the light. They also use logs, boulders, weed beds, and other sheltering features to evade sunlight. If the water is very clear, walleye will simply lie directly on the bottom, even if the prevailing temperature is not ideal. In turbid waters, walleye may feed in casual, slow-moving schools throughout the day. They are often found together with other prominent predators such as northern pike, smallmouth bass, and muskellunge. Their prey includes just about any available fish, including the various species of perch, drum, ciscoe, sucker, whitefish, shiners, chub, shad, bass, and even other walleye. Walleye are not above taking invertebrates either, such as crayfish, snails, or various insects.

Spawning occurs in spring or early summer on shallow shoals or in rivers. During summer, walleye generally remain close to their preferred, sheltered habitat. Their habitat and feeding patterns remain relatively unchanged during winter, and walleye are a very popular species for ice fishermen.

FISHING TACKLE Walleye have long been a favorite of anglers who can employ a wide variety of hardware to catch them. Wobbling plugs, such as the Rapala, Beno, or Flatfish, are widely used, especially while trolling over shallow structures or casting into faster-moving rivers. In deeper structures, crank baits, such as the Rapala Shad Rap or the Rattlin' Rap, are ideal.

Spinners, such as the Mepps Aglia or Blue Fox Vibrax, are also effective walleye baits, especially when they are worked near the bottom. Ice fishermen routinely employ special jigging spoons, such as the Swedish Pimple, Mr. Champ, or Rapala Pilkie Spoon. The most popular lures for walleye are jigs. These come in a variety of shapes and sizes and are especially potent in fast-moving and deeper water. Spoons, such as the Daredevle or

Walleye are notorious "tail hitters" and will sometimes fail to strike with sufficient determination to become hooked. When this occurs, try rigging a baited trailer hook to your spoon or jig to draw a more vigorous response from the fish. *Live-bait presentations, too, can be similarly improved by tying a short length of monofilament to the hook and then tying on a second hook, which can be embedded farther down the body of a minnow, worm, or leech.*

Little Cleo, can also be effective in faster-moving water.

FISHING TECHNIQUES Walleye can be taken by anglers using a wide variety of fishing styles. The most-often-used method is perhaps live bait-fishing. Most bait-fishermen use worms, minnows, leeches, or even frogs, cast either from shore or from a boat. Minnows are effective all year but especially during winter and spring. Worms and leeches are most often used in late spring and summer. Bait-fishermen should remember that a *lively* bait is a must and that walleye are notoriously light takers whose delicate strike can go unnoticed by the unwary angler.

Trolling with artificial lures is another popular method of catching walleye. The appropriate plug, spoon, or spinner is run over or alongside holding structures such as weed beds, river mouths, dropping shorelines, islands, or shoals.

Anglers usually cast for walleye at warm-water outflows of hydroelectric generating stations, waterfalls, dams, river mouths, or deep sections of rivers. Lures such as spoons, casting plugs, spinners, and jigs should generally be worked slowly and close to the bottom. Casting for walleye often involves frustration since the lure presentation must be "slow and deep," which means the lure frequently snags on the bottom. Jigs should be allowed to actually hit bottom before a lift-drop-lift-drop retrieve is begun by twitching the fishing rod. Many casting lures can be complemented with live bait such as a spinner-worm combination.

The ice fisherman uses two basic methods for taking walleye once he has actually located the fish, often by using sonar gear rigged through the hole in the ice. Fish are often found near weed lines, in channels, or near shoals, and tip up rigs are often used with one or two minnows as bait. When the fish are not concentrated, the ice fisherman will often switch to a jigging presentation, using various artificial lures tipped with minnows to attract stray or cruising fish.

Even the fly-fisherman can fish for walleye, especially when they are in more shallow water.

White Bass

COMMON NAMES bar blane (French), sand bass, silver bass, striper, white bass

DESCRIPTION The white bass is a member of the *Percichthyidae* or temperate bass family, along with the white perch, yellow bass, and striped bass. In fact, during the 1960s, fisheries biologists produced a very successful hybrid, which was stocked in reservoirs in the southern United States, by crossing male white bass with female striped bass. The white bass is silvery in color with a tinge of yellow on the underside. Its two dorsal fins are not quite connected, and its body is fairly compressed and rounded, giving it the appearance of an upright disk. Although it is quite similar to the yellow bass, it can be distinguished by the slightly protruding lower jaws, the ten or so continuous dark stripes running along the length of the body, and the fact that it has a delicate set of teeth on the base of the tongue.

SIZE White bass are a schooling fish. Members of the school tend to be the same size. If the angler has been taking fish of 3/4 of a pound for some time and suddenly begins to catch fish of 1 1/2 pounds, he can be fairly sure that a new school has moved in. Most white bass caught with rod and reel average between a 1/2 and 1 1/2 pounds. White bass seldom live longer than six years and rarely attain great size, although in large, southern bodies of water containing a large forage base of shad they may routinely grow to weigh 3 or more pounds. The world-record white bass was caught in just such a southern body

FOR FISH LOVERS, SILVERS ARE GREAT EATING.

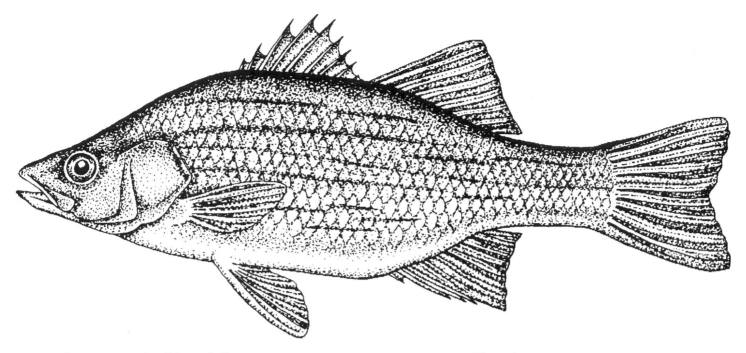

of water in the United States. This unusually large fish weighed 6 pounds, 13 ounces and was taken in Lake Orange, Virginia. In Canada, a 3.02-pound white bass was taken on a nightcrawler from the warm-water outflow in Pickering, Ontario.

DISTRIBUTION In the United States, white bass range from the St. Lawrence through the Great Lakes and westward to South Dakota. Their southern range extends all the way south to the Gulf states of Texas, Louisiana, Mississippi, and Alabama. This American range has constantly been expanded through highly successful transplanting programs.

In Canada, the white bass has long been firmly entrenched in Lake Ontario, Lake Erie, the Detroit River, Lake St. Clair, Lake Huron, and Lake Nipissing. This somewhat limited range has recently been extended into Quebec and the St. Lawrence River. An isolated pocket of white bass have even managed to take hold in Lake Winnipeg, Manitoba, possibly via the Red River.

BEHAVIOR AND HABITAT The white bass is an exclusively freshwater species that has been extensively transplanted, especially to large reservoirs that regularly produce spectacular white-bass fishing. The ideal habitat for this species seems to be large bodies of water of 300 or

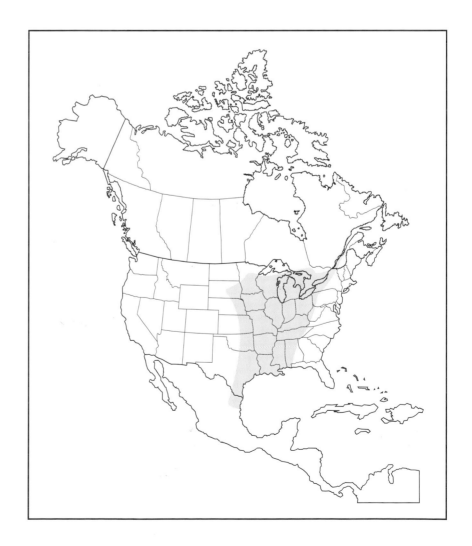

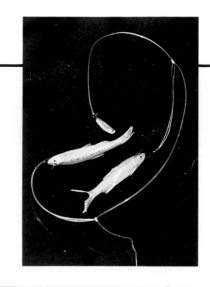
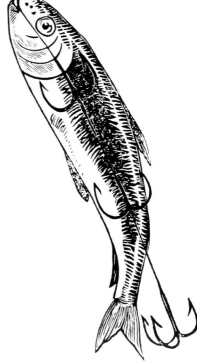

more acres such as large lakes or reservoirs, particularly those connected by large river systems. Although they can live in turbid water, they prefer clear water with bottom consisting of sand, gravel, or rock. In contrast to other fish, such as the crappies, white bass are often found in open water at depths ranging from 10 to 30 feet. Spawning occurs during a five- to ten-day period in the spring, from April to July, depending on location. White bass will congregate in great numbers to spawn at the mouths of tributary streams and rivers and provide excellent sport for anglers. Spawning occurs in water temperatures between 58 and 64 degrees Fahrenheit in approximately 6 feet of water. The parents do not build nests and do not guard their eggs, which may exceed 500,000 in number. After spawning, the white bass move in schools back into the river mouths of the spawning tributary. After a few days or weeks they will then gradually move back into the main lake. During summer, white bass schools may move about frequently and independently of temperature strata or underwater structure. Frequently, however, they can be located along break-lines such as creek channels, depressions, or underwater ridges. During summer and fall, white bass are famous for their "en masse" attacks on schools of bait fish such as shad. The water surface may actually appear to "boil" with desperately jumping shad and the slicing dorsal fins of the feeding bass. Besides feeding on fish, including other perch-family members, white bass will also snap up insect larvae and various crustaceans. The best locations for feeding white bass are sand or gravel flats near deep water, river mouths, sunken islands, or even piers and bridge abutments. During the winter, white bass will feed very little when water temperature drops below 50 degrees Fahrenheit, and the best bet for anglers is to look for them near warm-water outflows, such as those of generating stations.

FISHING TACKLE As is the case with most panfish, white bass will strike a variety of baits and lures as long as

1 When fishing for white bass, use tiny crank baits to locate the fish. Once you've located them, use spoons, spinners, and jigs to catch one fish after another.

2 White bass usually move around in tight schools consist-ing of fish of the same size. If the fish you're getting are all small, move around and try to find another school that has bigger fish.

3 You can double your pleasure and your results when fishing for white bass if you tie a dropper onto your line and attach another lure like a fly or jig. "Two is often better than one."

4 Because light line is best for white bass, it's doubly important to sharpen your hooks.

---

they are sized to fit into their small mouths. Small spinners along the lines of a Shyster or Cottontail are often used, as well as small spoons such as the Hopkins Shorty or Mepps Spoon. Wobbling plugs such as the Bo-Jack, Tail Gasper, Little George, or the various Rapalas are also very successful. Since white bass prefer deeper water, often with rocky bottoms, jigs are quite rightly a good choice, including such old reliables as the standard rainbow or bucktail jigs, as well as newcomers like the Whistler or the Road Runner.

FISHING TECHNIQUES When white bass are spawning they are conveniently concentrated for the shore fisherman. The tail sections of flows below dams are natural hot-spots for these fish, and the angler can literally land dozens and dozens of fish each day when the run is in. If these spawning fish ignore spinners or spoons, as they will sometimes do, a tiny 1/16 ounce jig or even a jig tipped with bait may bring them to life. Spawning white bass may also be found in stands of flooded brush, in log jams, and in the eddies of small clear creeks, flowing into known white-bass lakes or reservoirs.

In large lakes, anglers often keep on the lookout for large schools of white bass feeding on panicky schools of bait fish. When such a feeding school has been sighted, anglers repeatedly cast shallow-running lures into the surface commotion until the fish finally retreat. Often they are then vertically fished with jigging lures such as spoons or jigs. Another popular method for taking white bass is night fishing. During spawning runs or in the doldrums of mid-summer, special lighted floats are used, using either lithium batteries or cyalume light sticks. These are fished with minnows along lighted bridges, piers, and docks, as well as near river channels, river mouths, and sand flats.

When white bass are in deep water they are best located with the aid of electronic sonar gear. In summer they will often be found suspended in 30 feet of water, and, in late fall, they may seek out the warmer water at depths of 50 or more feet.

DAMS ARE GREAT HOLDING AREAS FOR SPRINGTIME BASS.

Glossary

This glossary explains and defines some of the technical words and terms used in this book. Note that the definitions given apply to fishing only, and may differ from standard dictionary definitions in some instances.

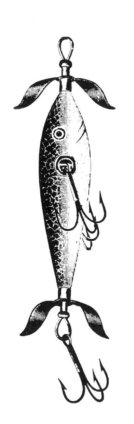

ACTION The behavior of a rod under load while fighting a fish or casting, often described in terms of the rate of a blank's taper, e.g., slow, medium, or fast. The blank is the tubular shaft comprising the main part of a fishing rod.

AMBUSH The act of lying in wait for or of attacking by surprise from a concealed position.

ANADROMOUS Fish that move from salt water to fresh water. Usually fish will spawn in fresh water, then spend the rest of their adult life in salt water.

BACK-TROLLING A popular technique to use when fishing for walleye. The engine is placed in reverse gear and the angler trolls backward. This technique gives the angler total control over his speed and maneuvers.

BAIT CASTERS Any rods that have pistol grips or trigger grips designed to be used with bait-casting reels. These reels will have a level-wind or center-wind line pickup mechanism and are designed to be operated with the thumb and hand when casting.

BAIT FISH Minnows, alewives, freshwater herring, and smelt that are commonly eaten by game fish.

BEND The bend in a river, where the river makes a directional turn and current is channeled and increased. Bends usually have deeper water and undercut banks.

BOTTOM-WALKING WEIGHTS Fishing weights that have a wire frame in a "V" configuration with a banana-shaped sinker molded on one end. These sinkers are designed to bump along the bottom and are snagproof.

BUCKTAIL Deer hair from a deer's tail, commonly used when tying dry flies or bucktail jigs.

CANNONBALL Large lead weight, usually ranging from 6 to 12 pounds, that is attached to the wire cable of a downrigger used to troll lures in deep water.

CAST The art of throwing a line.

CAUDAL PEDUNCLE The narrow part of a fish's body just in front of the tail, often called the "tail wrist."

COARSE FISH Most warm-water fish that are not considered game fish are commonly called coarse fish. These include: suckers, carp, catfish, and various species of panfish.

COLD FRONT Sudden drops in temperature of ten degrees or more after a stretch of moderate to warm temperatures would be considered a "cold front." Some cold fronts last a matter of hours; some last for days. Cold fronts are usually produced by a high-pressure system suddenly moving in on a low-pressure system.

COOL WATER Walleye cannot tolerate constant water temperatures over 80 degrees Fahrenheit. Maximum high, cold-water temperatures would generally not exceed 75 degrees.

"COUNT-DOWN" RAPALA A weighted wobbling lure that has been designed to be used with a "count-down" technique. The fisherman casts the lure and, when it hits the water, he starts counting as it drops. This method is mostly used when trying to locate suspended fish.

COVER Something that protects, shelters, or guards. A place of natural shelter for a fish to hide for security or as a place of ambush. Cover can be made of rocks, wood, weeds, and even surface turbulence.

CRANK The technique used to retrieve a deep-diving or shallow-running plug. The angler has to continuously crank or reel in the lure to give it proper action.

CRUSTACEAN Animals that are mostly aquatic in nature, with hard outer shells, such as crayfish, water fleas, and other aquatic arthropods.

CURRENT BREAK An area in the water where fast-flowing water meets slow-moving or still water. Current breaks are usually produced when bottom structures protrude up from the bottom or where other obstructions force the current in a certain direction. High winds and seiche movement in a lake can produce currents and current breaks.

DEADFALL Dead trees that have fallen into the water.

DOWNRIGGER A mechanism that consists of a flexible arm, a large reel, a lead cannonball, and wire line that is used to deliver a fisherman's line and lure to a desired depth.

DOWNRIGGER FISHING A fishing technique in which a downrigger is used in conjunction with a cannonball, wire line, and a release to deliver the fisherman's bait to a desired depth.

DRAG A reel mechanism that is designed to apply pressure on the line as a fish is taking it out. Most drags can be manually adjusted for desired tension.

DRESSED JIG A jig that either has hair or bucktail tied to it, or that is used with a rubber grub body.

DROP-OFF A rapid vertical change in bottom depth from shallow to deep water.

DROPPER A length of line that can be added to the main monofilament line or leader, often used when adding a second fly or jig to the line.

DRY FLY A fly intended to float on or in the surface layer of the water.

EUTROPHIC A lake rich in dissolved nutrients, shallow and with seasonal oxygen deficiency in the hypolimnion, the stagnant layer of water beneath the thermocline.

FALL TURNOVER An occurrence in a lake when the surface water becomes colder then the warmer water below. Because of its higher density, the colder water drops and mixes with the warmer water. This usually happens across Canada between October and November, prior to "ice-up."

FISH FINDER A type of electronic equipment that enables a fisherman to detect the presence of fish in the water below the boat. A transducer and a receiver with a screen are the two main components of a fish finder. Most fish finders require a 12-volt battery as their power source.

FLASHER A type of fish finder that gets its name from the way in which it relays information to the angler. Depth readings and fish are recorded as light flashes on a screen.

FLAT A feature in a lake or river where the bottom is consistently shallower than the surrounding water. Flats are usually created when sediments, such as soil, silt, or other deposits, build up in a given area. Strong winds and currents account for most of the flats existing in a given body of water; therefore, flats are usually located near river channels, river mouths, and wind-blown ends of lakes.

FLIPPING A fishing technique developed for catching largemouth bass. The angler drops or "flips" his bait along undercut banks, holes in weedbeds, and along weed edges.

FLIPPING RODS These rods are usually 7 1/2 to 8 feet long. They have a long butt, are equipped with a "trigger" reel seat, and are designated as "heavy-action" rods to be used with 20- to 40-pound-test line. These rods are usually semi-telescopic, allowing the main part of the rod blank to collapse into the lower part of the rod blank near the reel seat and butt area.

FLOAT RIG A technique where a buoyant float is used above the bait to keep the bait suspended off the bottom.

FLOATING JIG HEAD A jig head that is made out of a buoyant material such as cork or foam. These types of jigs will suspend live bait off the bottom.

FOOD SHELF An area in a lake or river where there is a rich nutrient supply that stimulates fish and plant growth.

FORAGE The food consumed by fish.

FREE-SPOOLING When a person casts with a bait-casting reel, he engages a release mechanism that allows the spool to roll freely, permitting the line to go out.

HATCH Insects that are evolving from their nymph stage to their flying-insect stage. Insect hatches usually occur on the surface when air and water temperatures start to rise.

HEAD A location on a stream or river. The head area of a river is located at the beginning of a pool where the rapids change to flowing deeper water.

HEAVY ACTION The stiffness of a fishing rod. Fishing rods that are designed to be used with 15- to 30-pound-test line and with lures weighing between 1/4 and 1 1/2 ounces are classified as heavy action.

HOLES Holes are the deepest areas in rivers and lakes.

HOOTCHIE A plastic or rubber squid-imitating lure commonly used on the west coast for a variety of game fish species.

HOT-SPOT An area in a river, stream, or lake where there is a concentration of fish that can be readily caught.

ICE-OUT The period when the ice that covers a frozen lake melts or is blown along the shoreline, creating open water.

INACTIVE A phase when fish are in a lethargic mood. At this time they will be stationary or close to the bottom of a given body of water.

JERK BAIT A large lure commonly used for muskies. Its name comes from the method of retrieval, which consists of a sharp jerking motion.

JIG A type of lure usually featuring a lead head and single hook upon which various man-made or natural materials are attached to represent a variety of forage for fish.

KYPE A hook-like mass of cartilage protruding from the lower jaw of male salmonid species of fish, usually developed prior to spawning.

LATERAL LINE A longitudinal line along each side of the body of most fishes that is usually distinguished by dash-like marks or differently colored scales. The lateral line contains the openings of the lateral line organ, which a fish uses to detect vibrations.

LEAD The line distance between a cannonball and the fisherman's lure.

LIE An area away from the main current in a river or stream commonly used by fish to hold while feeding or resting.

LIGHT ACTION Light action is used to define rods that are designed to be used with 4- to 8-pound-test line and with lures weighing from 1/8 to 1/4 ounces.

LINE DIAMETER The thickness of the outside surface of any fishing line. Line diameter is usually measured in thousands of an inch.

LIVE BAIT RIGS These rigs are made up of a piece of monofilament line to act as a leader, a single bait-holding hook, and a sliding sinker. They are designed to be used with live bait that can be fished on the bottom or suspended off the bottom with the use of a flotation device attached near the hook.

LIVE WELL An aerated holding tank built into modern fishing boats to keep bait or fish alive.

MEDIUM ACTION Rods that are designed to be used with 10- to 14-pound-test line and with lures weighing 1/4 to 1/2 ounces.

MEZO A lake that shows eutrophic and oligotrophic characteristics.

NEUTRAL A phase fish are in when they can be induced to strike. When fish are "neutral," they will move to attack a bait.

NOODLE RODS These rods are normally 12 to 14 feet in length and have a very light action. They are designed to be used with very light line between 2- and 4-pound-test.

NYMPH The aquatic stage of many flying insects.

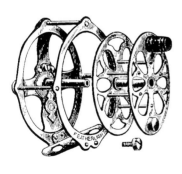

OLIGOTROPHIC Lakes that have a deficiency in plant nutrients, an abundance of dissolved oxygen, and no stratification.

PARR Young salmonids still residing in the stream or river habitat.

PATTERN A set of tactics and types of locations on a lake that an angler establishes to consistently produce fish. A log will help you to easily identify your recorded data and in turn construct a strategy. Include things such as appropriate tackle, presentation, fishing locations, and other pertinent data.

PATTERN (fly fishing) The arrangements of different fly-tying materials when tying a fly. Certain patterns of material are used to tie specific flies.

PATTERN FISHING Pattern fishing is looking for similar water conditions with certain common elements that have produced fish under identical conditions at different locations on a given body of water.

POCKETS Small, deeper sections in a stream or lake.

POST-SPAWN The time period right after spawning when fish are preparing themselves for their normal seasonal activity.

PRESENTATION The manner in which you present live bait or an artificial lure in front of a fish to make it strike.

REDD A bed or nest made by spawning fish.

REEFS A chain, mass, or ridge of rocks or sand lying at or near the surface of the water.

RIFFLES Sections of shallow, fast water where the surface water comes in contact with the main stream bottom.

RIP-JIGGING A jigging technique that is used when fishing very thick weed areas. The angler casts his jig out and allows it to fall to the bottom. When the jig settles, the fisherman snaps the rod back, making the jig cut right through aquatic vegetation, and then he lets the jig fall to the bottom again. This procedure is repeated over and over again until a fish strikes.

ROD BLANK The main shaft of the fishing rod onto which the guides, handle, and reel seat are attached.

ROD BUTT The lower section of a fishing rod that contains the reel seat.

ROD SENSITIVITY How sensitive a rod tip is when relaying vibrations or movement by the fishing line. Graphite rods will be much more sensitive than fiberglass rods.

ROE Fish eggs (commonly used as bait by trout and salmon anglers).

RUN Areas in a river where the water flows at a consistent speed and depth.

SLIDING FLOAT RIGS A float with a hole through the center is rigged along with a piece of living rubber material above the hook and sinker. The float can run freely up and down the line between the rubber stopper and the sinkers. The rubber stopper is adjustable and runs through the guides and onto the reel. This makes for easy casting because the float slides to the sinkers. When it hits the water, the float allows the line to run through it until it reaches the rubber stopper.

SLOT LIMITS Regulations permitting anglers to keep fish that measure either under or over a particular size. This is usually designed to protect medium- to large-sized fish for spawning purposes but allowing small fish or trophy fish to be harvested.

SMOLT Young Atlantic salmon that migrate to sea.

SNAP A mechanism that is tied to the end of a fisherman's line. It allows the angler to change lures without having to retie them each time. Snaps are usually constructed of thin wire material. They can be purchased individually or attached to a swivel.

SNAP-JIGGING Another expression for rip-jigging.

SNAP-SWIVEL This mechanism would be classified as terminal tackle. A snap-swivel is attached to the end of the fishing line and is used to change lures without cutting the line each time.

SPAWN The stage when fish, amphibians, or other aquatic animals deposit their eggs as part of their reproductive cycle.

SPIN-CASTING Two-piece rods with pistol grips that are designed to be used with push-button closed-faced reels.

SPLIT SHOT Small round weights that are attached to the line.

STAINED WATER Certain types of suspended materials in water can give water a particular color. In many areas, bottom type and water turbulence can create "tea colored" water. Stained water is usually influenced by the aquatic vegetation growth in a given lake and the type of sediments found on the bottom of the lake.

STILL FISHING Fishing from a stationary spot with live bait either on bottom or suspended without intentionally moving the bait.

STREAMCRAFT The art of reading and analyzing a stream environment in order to successfully catch fish.

STREAMER Flies that are designed to imitate minnows or small baitfish.

STRIKE ZONE The imaginary area around a fish, representing the territory within which it will feed. The strike zone will vary in size, depending on the fishes' activity. Inactive fish have a small or nonexistent strike zone; feeding fish will have a large strike zone and will move several feet to take a bait.

STRUCTURE A sudden change of 5 feet or more in bottom depth over a short distance. Such a change is usually created by shorelines, points, islands, rockpiles, bars, reefs, shoals, or dropoffs.

TAIL A section of river or stream that is located immediately after the main pool and just before the next rapids. The "tail" of a pool is characterized by slick, flat, and fast surface water that turns into rapids.

TAILING Landing a fish by grabbing it by the "caudal peduncle."

TAILING GLOVE Specialized glove used to grab the "caudal peduncle" of a fish.

TAPETUM LUCIDUM A light-sensitive layer of skin that covers the eye of a walleye.

TERMINAL TACKLE All non-lure fishing accessories that are attached to the fishing line are terminal tackle. This includes weights, floats, hooks, snaps, snap-swivels, and leaders.

THERMOCLINE A layer of water, found at varying depths, in which the temperature decreases faster than in the layers above and below.

TURBID WATER Water that is not clear. Turbidity can be caused by suspended living matter such as algae and plankton or suspended organic sediments and soil.

TWITCHING A technique used when fishing a wobbling lure on the surface of the water. The fisherman casts the lure out, lets it settle on the surface, then retrieves, using a twitching action.

UNDERCUT Section of land that meets the water where the water has eroded the soil below the surface. "Undercut" banks are common in bends of rivers and along east-facing shorelines.

UNDERWATER POINT Shoreline points that extend into deeper water. Most of the time, these major structures can be located only with a fish finder.

UNDRESSED JIG A jig made up of a jig hook with a molded lead head that is bare. These jigs are usually used with live bait or are "dressed" with hair, bucktail, or rubber materials.

ULTRA-LIGHT Any rod that is very flexible and designed to be used with 2- to 4-pound-test line and with lures weighing between 1/16 and 1/8 ounce would be classified as "ultra-light" in action.

VERTICAL JIGGING This technique works well when fishing in deeper water. Line is released so that a lure will fall to the bottom. When the lure is suspended near the bottom, the line is drawn tight. The fisherman lifts his rod up, lifting the spoon off the bottom, then letting the spoon "free-fall" back to its bottom position. The depth of the spoon and the length of the "jig lifts" is varied until the fisherman comes up with a productive combination.

WALLEYE RIG A manufactured live-bait rig that uses monofilament line and allows the fisherman to use two baits, one above the other, suspended under a float or right on the bottom.

WEED LINE A weed bed with a defined weed edge constitutes a weed line. Weed lines usually appear as a border of vegetation that meets open water.

WET FLY A fly designed to sink beneath the surface of the water.

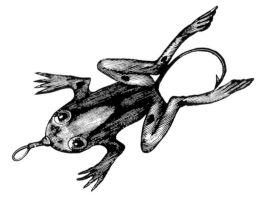

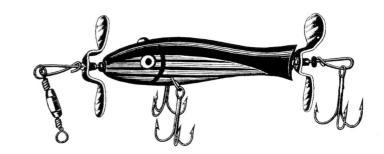

Ind.

Acipenser fulvescens
Acipenser transmor
Adams River, B.
Air-bladder sw
Aluminum b
Ambloplites r
Anadromo
Angling:
  18; fish
  14-1
Arcti
Arc
At'
A

  .s, 80

  .ing methods, 10-12
  .d, 170-73

  .ow trout, 86, 134-37.
  See also Steelhead
Redbreast sunfish, 170-73
Redd, 35
Redear sunfish, 170-73
Redfin pickerel, 120-23
Reels and rods. *See* Fishing tackle
Rig: attractor added to, 118; float jigging
  technique, 105; for Sauger, 144;
  lake-trout trolling, 105; quick-strike,
  23-24, 128
River fish, 22
Rock bass, 138-41
Roe bags, 74, 132
Ross Swimmer Tail, 76

Salmo clarki, 84
Salmo salar, 42
Salmo trutta, 53
Salmon, 25, 30-31
  Atlantic, 42-47
  Chinook, 64-69
  Chum, 70-74
  Coho, 75-79
  Great Lakes, 66-67
  Kokanee, 49, 96-99, 153
  landlocked, 42-43
  Pink, 130-33
  Sockeye, 96, 152-57
Salvelinus alpinus, 34
Salvelinus fontinalis, 48
Salvelinus malma, 88
Salvelinus namaycush, 100-05
Santee-Cooper Reservoir, 59
Sauger, 142-45

  oass, 141; Striped
  White bass, 178, 180-81
  est, 20

  .sh, 28
  .ctic char, 34
Arctic grayling, 38-39
Atlantic salmon, 42
Brook trout, 49
Brown trout, 53
Channel catfish, 58-59
Chinook salmon, 64-65
Chum salmon, 70
Coho salmon, 75
Crappie, 80
Cutthroat trout, 84
Dolly Varden, 88-89
Inconnu, 92
Kokanee, 96
Lake trout, 100-01
Largemouth bass, 106
Muskellunge, 110-11
Perch, 114-15
Pickerel, 120
Pike, 124-25
Pink salmon, 130
Rainbow trout, 134-35
Rock bass, 138
Sauger, 142
Smallmouth bass, 147
Sockeye salmon, 153
Steelhead, 158-59
Striped bass, 162
Sturgeon, 166
Sunfish, 170-71
Walleye, 174-75
White bass, 178-79
Slime coating on fish, 25
Smallmouth bass, 29-30, 146-51
Sockeye salmon, 152-57
Sonar, 18, 102, 168, 181
Spawn bags, 160
Spawning
  Atlantic salmon, 42-44
  Brook trout, 50
  Brown trout, 54-55
  Channel catfish, 59
  Chinook salmon, 64-67
  Chum salmon, 71-72
  Coho salmon, 76, 79
  Crappie, 81-82
  Cutthroat trout, 85
  Inconnu, 94
  Kokanee, 97-98

Lake trout, 101-02
Pickerel, 121-22
Pike, 126
Pink salmon, 131-32
Rock bass, 139-40
Sauger, 143
Sockeye salmon, 152-54
Striped bass, 163
Sturgeon, 167-69
Walleye, 176
White bass, 180-81
White perch, 116
Yellow perch, 118
Spinners
  Arctic char, 36
  Arctic grayling, 40-41
  Brown trout, 57
  Dolly Varden, 90, 91
  Kokanee, 99
  Rainbow trout, 136
Splake, 48
Spoons: Coho, 76, 78; Dolly Varden, 91;
  Pickerel, 123
Stackers, 78
Steelhead, 158-61. *See also* Rainbow
  trout
Stenodus leucichthys, 92
Stizostedion canadense, 142
Stizostedion vitreum, 174
"Stream craft," 52
Stream fish, 30-31, 48-52
Stress: live release, 22, 28, 29
Strikes: Muskellunge, 111-12;
  Pickerel, 122; Salmon, 46, 47
Striped bass, 162-65
Sturgeon, 166-69
Sunfish, 170-73
Super Release Dodger, 157
Survival rate: live release, 22

Tailing glove, 25, 154
"Taking lies," 45, 46
Tapetum lucidum, 143
Teeth of bass, 29
Temperature gauges and probes, 18
Thermocline, 116
Thymallus arcticus, 38
Time to fish
  Brown trout, 56-57
  Channel catfish, 60, 62
  Crappie, 82, 83
  Cutthroat trout, 87
  Inconnu, 95
  Lake trout, 104
  Largemouth bass, 109

Muskellunge, 112
Perch, 119
Smallmouth bass, 150
Sockeye salmon, 154
Steelhead, 160-61
Striped bass, 164, 165
White bass, 181
Treatyse of Fishing with an Angle, 12
Trolling
  Brown trout, 55, 56
  Chinook salmon, 67, 69
  Coho salmon, 77-79
  Kokanee, 98-99
  Lake trout, 102, 104-05
  Pike, 129
  Sauger, 144
  Sockeye salmon, 157
  Striped bass, 164
  Walleye, 177
Trout
  Brook, 48-52
  Brown, 53-57
  catch and release, 25, 30-31
  Cutthroat, 84-87
  Lake, 100-05
  Rainbow, 86, 134-37
  Steelhead, 158-61
  Tiger, 48
Turbid water, 143, 145, 175-76, 180
Twitching, 148

Vermiculations, 48

Walleye, 30, 120, 174-77.
  See also Sauger
Wedding Band spinners, 98
Weight. *See* Size
White bass, 178-81
White crappie, 80-83
Whitefish, 92-95
White perch, 114-19
White sturgeon, 166-69
Wire leaders, 128
Worms, 119

Yellow perch, 114-19